KU-677-715

OVERCOMING TRAUMATIC STRESS

A self-help guide using cognitive behavioral techniques

Claudia Herbert
and
Ann Wetmore

177766x

LIBRARY

ACC. No. 36021567   DEPT.

CLASS No. 616.8521 BRE

WITHDRAWN

UNIVERSITY
OF CHESTER

NEW YORK UNIVERSITY PRESS
Washington Square, New York

First published in the U.S.A. in 2001 by
New York University Press
Washington Square, New York, NY 10003

Copyright © Claudia Herbert and Ann Wetmore 1999, 2001

The rights of Claudia Herbert and Ann Wetmore to be identified as
authors of this work have been asserted by them in accordance with the
Copyright, Designs and Patents Act, 1988, 2001

Lines from 'Sometimes' by Sheenagh Pugh are taken
from *Selected Poems* published by Seren, UK, and used with kind
permission of the publishers.

All rights reserved. No part of this publication may be
reproduced in any form or by any means without the prior
written permission of the publisher.

Library of Congress Cataloging-in-Publication Data

Herbert, Claudia
Overcoming Traumatic Stress: a self-help guide using cognitive
behavioral techniques/ Claudia Herbert and Ann Wetmore.
p. cm. – (Overcoming series)
originally published: London: Robinson Pub., 1999.
Includes bibliographical references and index.
ISBN 0-8147-3628-9 (pbk.: alk.paper)
1. Post-traumatic stress disorder. 2. Cognitive therapy. 3. Self-help techniques.
I. Wetmore, Ann. II Title. III Series.

RC552.P67 H 465 2001
616.85'21   00-067000

Important Note

This book is not intended to be a substitute for any medical advice or
treatment. Any person with a condition requiring medical attention
should consult a qualified medical practitioner or suitable therapist.

Printed and bound in Great Britain

To my children, to Ulf and to Martina,
being the people in this world who are dearest to me.

C.H.

For Morgan O'Connell and James Thompson,
wonderful teachers, who welcomed an eager
Canadian into their trauma centres.

A.W.

Contents

Introduction

Introduction

Acknowledgements

I would like to thank all those who have supported, guided and taught me both throughout my personal and my professional life, without whose input I would not have been able to achieve what I have so far. I am especially appreciative of all the support, encouragement and nurturing that I received throughout the writing of this book from my partner, Ulf Jarisch. Above all, however, I would like to thank my clients, who have allowed me, during their course of therapy, to travel with them and join them a little way along each of their own individual life paths. This has made me feel very privileged and without it I would not be able to know what I now know or be the therapist that I now am.

Claudia Herbert

I wish to acknowledge, with gratitude, two grants from the British Council (Canada), which enabled me to undertake the initial work on this project in 1991 and 1992. Dr Morgan O'Connell at the Royal Navy Hospital Haslar, and Dr James Thompson, of the Traumatic Stress Clinic, Middlesex Hospital, London, were tremendously helpful. I am also grateful to Dean Carol Hill, Mount Saint Vincent University, Halifax, Nova Scotia, for supporting my frequent requests for research leaves. To all the gifted individuals at the Traumatic Stress Clinic, with whom I have had the pleasure to be associated, I extend my deepest respect. To Dr Steven Bruhm, who patiently translated so many docu-

Acknowledgements

ments, to my family and many friends, who extended support in a multitude of kindnesses, I gratefully applaud you.

Ann Wetmore

Introduction

Why cognitive behavior therapy?

Over the past two or three decades, there has been something of a revolution in the field of psychological treatment. Freud and his followers had a major impact on the way in which psychological therapy was conceptualized, and psychoanalysis and psychodynamic psychotherapy dominated the field for the first half of this century. So, long-term treatments were offered which were designed to uncover the childhood roots of personal problems – offered, that is, to those who could afford it. There was some attempt by a few health service practitioners with a public conscience to modify this form of treatment (by, for example, offering short-term treatment or group therapy), but the demand for help was so great that this had little impact. Also, whilst numerous case histories can be found of people who are convinced that psychotherapy did help them, practitioners of this form of therapy showed remarkably little interest in demonstrating that what they were offering their patients was, in fact, helpful.

As a reaction to the exclusivity of psychodynamic therapies and the slender evidence for its usefulness, in the 1950s and 1960s a set of techniques was developed, broadly collectively termed 'behavior therapy'. These techniques shared two basic features. First, they aimed to remove symptoms (such as anxiety) by dealing with those symptoms themselves, rather than their deep-seated underlying historical causes. Second, they were techniques, loosely related to what laboratory psychologists were

xiii

finding out about the mechanisms of learning, which were formulated in testable terms. Indeed, practitioners of behavior therapy were committed to using techniques of proven value or, at worst, of a form which could potentially be put to the test. The area where these techniques proved of most value was in the treatment of anxiety disorders, especially specific phobias (such as fear of animals or of heights) and agoraphobia, both notoriously difficult to treat using conventional psychotherapies.

After an initial flush of enthusiasm, discontent with behavior therapy grew. There were a number of reasons for this, an important one of which was the fact that behavior therapy did not deal with the internal thoughts which were so obviously central to the distress that patients were experiencing. In this context, the fact that behavior therapy proved so inadequate when it came to the treatment of depression highlighted the need for major revision. In the late 1960s and early 1970s a treatment was developed specifically for depression called 'cognitive therapy'. The pioneer in this enterprise was an American psychiatrist, Professor Aaron T. Beck, who developed a theory of depression which emphasized the importance of people's depressed styles of thinking. He also specified a new form of therapy. It would not be an exaggeration to say that Beck's work has changed the nature of psychotherapy, not just for depressions but for a range of psychological problems.

In recent years the cognitive techniques introduced by Beck have been merged with the techniques developed earlier by the behavior therapists to produce a body of theory and practice which has come to be known as 'cognitive behavior therapy'. There are two reasons why this form of treatment has come to be so important within the field of psychotherapy. First, cognitive therapy for depression, as originally described by Beck and developed by his successors, has been subjected to the strictest scientific testing; and it has been found to be a highly successful treatment for a significant proportion of cases of depression. Not only has it proved to be as effective as the best alternative treatments (except in the most severe cases, where medication is required), but some studies suggest that people treated successfully with cognitive behavior therapy are less likely to experience a later recurrence of their depression than people treated successfully with other forms of therapy (such as antidepressant medication). Second, it has become clear that specific patterns of thinking are associated with a range of psychological problems and that treatments which deal with these styles of thinking are highly effective. So, specific cognitive behavioral treatments have been developed for anxiety disorders, like panic disorder, generalized anxiety disorder, specific phobias and social phobia, obsessive compulsive disorders, and hypochondriasis (health anxiety), as well as for other conditions such as compulsive gambling, alcohol and drug addiction, and eating disorders like bulimia nervosa and binge-eating disorder. Indeed, cognitive behavorial techniques have a wide application beyond the narrow categories of psychological disorders: they have been applied effectively, for example, to helping people with low self-esteem and those with marital difficulties.

At any one time almost 10 per cent of the general population is suffering from depression, and more than 10 per cent has one or other of the anxiety disorders. Many others have a range of psychological problems and personal difficulties. It is of the greatest importance that treatments of proven effectiveness are developed. However, even when the armoury of therapies is, as it were, full, there remains a very great problem – namely that the delivery of treatment is expensive and the resources are not going to be available evermore. Whilst this shortfall could be met by lots of people helping themselves, commonly the natural inclination to make oneself feel better in the present is to do precisely those things which perpetuate or even exacerbate one's problems. For example, the person with agoraphobia will stay at home to prevent the possibility of an anxiety attack; and the person with bulimia nervosa will avoid eating all potentially fattening foods. Whilst such strategies might resolve some immediate crisis, they leave the underlying problem intact and provide no real help in dealing with future difficulties.

So, there is a twin problem here: although effective treatments have been developed, they are not widely available; and when people try to help themselves they often make matters worse. In recent years the community of cognitive behavior therapists have responded to this situation. What they have done is to take the principles and techniques of specific cognitive behavior therapies for particular problems and represent them in self-help manuals. These manuals specify a systematic program of treatment which the individual sufferer is advised to work through to overcome their difficulties. In this way, the cognitive behavioral therapeutic techniques of proven value are being made available on the widest possible basis.

Self-help manuals are never going to replace therapists. Many people will need individual treatment from a qualified therapist. It is also the case that, despite the widespread success of cognitive behavioral therapy, some people will not respond to it and will need one of the other treatments available. Nevertheless, although research on the use of cognitive behavioral self-help manuals is at an early stage, the work done to date indicates that for a very great many people such a manual will prove sufficient for them to overcome their problems without professional help.

Many people suffer silently and secretly for years. Sometimes appropriate help is not forthcoming despite their efforts to find it. Sometimes they feel too ashamed or guilty to reveal their problems to anyone. For many of these people the cognitive behavioral self-help manuals will provide a lifeline to recovery and a better future.

Professor Peter Cooper
The University of Reading

PART ONE

Understanding Traumatic Stress

When Trauma Strikes

In the Grip of Trauma

Terrible events are hard to deal with. Sudden, traumatic experiences can shatter people's lives and leave a profound mark on the way they feel about themselves and their lives. Traumas hurt! Often they not only cause terrible physical injuries but emotional injury as well, which can be far more painful and take much longer to heal. The effect of trauma can be a lingering feeling that your world has changed utterly.

Despite hearing or reading about terrible events all the time on the television, radio or newspaper, people often cannot really believe that such things could happen to them. You have probably felt relatively safe in your own world and at least felt you were able to cope with problems as they came along.

Suddenly, even little things can feel overwhelming and there is a sense that things are no longer within your control. It is as if your bubble of safety has burst. All the beliefs you held about yourself and your world before the trauma seem to have changed and are no longer felt to be true (Janoff-Bulman, 1992). You are in the Grip of Trauma!

What is a Traumatic Event?

Although everyone encounters many intensely upsetting and stressful situations during the course of their lives, not many of these would be considered *traumatic* events. *An experience can be described as traumatic when a person's normal ability to cope*

has been completely overwhelmed by a terrible event, such as the
one described below:

'On Saturday, 5 October 1997, 2 p.m. Francine picked up
her friend Jim to go for a walk in the woods. It was a lovely
and sunny autumn afternoon. As they were driving towards
the woods, Francine noticed that all the colors were so vivid
around them and despite the hint of cool air, which had
already turned some of the leaves brown, she thought that
this would be a lovely treat for them. They drove along a clear
stretch of country road, when she saw a car coming over the
brow of a hill some way ahead of them. She noticed that the
other car was starting to swerve and pull further and further
out onto their side of the road. She thought that the driver
must surely soon notice them and pull back into the other
lane. As she started to slow down, she felt her heart pounding. She heard Jim swearing from his passenger seat. The
driver of the other car didn't seem to have noticed them. He
didn't seem to be aware even that he was on the wrong side of
the road, heading straight towards their car. Thoughts started
to race through Francine's mind: Was he dead or had he
passed out? ... Should she pull over into the other lane? ...
But what if he had fallen asleep at the wheel and would wake
up to pull over onto his side of the road in the last minute?
He would drive into them and kill them. She thought that
she was too young to die ... she felt angry ... she felt terrified
... she wondered if she should pull over into the ditch on her
side of the road. But what if he drove straight into them there?
He didn't seem to wake up ... he was coming closer and closer
... she didn't want to die ... and then the bang, this awful
crushing noise of metal. She heard Jim scream and felt herself pulled up into the air, her head hit the inside of the roof
of her car. She felt dazed, confused and couldn't move ...
then she looked over to Jim ... he was totally slumped forward, he was moaning, blood trickled from his head. She heard
herself asking: Jim, Jim, are you alive, can you hear me? Stay
with it, stay alive! ... don't leave me!'

Francine

4

There are many ways in which traumas can occur. Usually, an event would be considered traumatic if *a person had experienced or been a witness to an event that involved actual or threatened death or serious injury*. There might also have been *a threat to this person's or other people's physical integrity*, so that they feared physical harm would come to them. This threat could have been so overwhelming that the person would have *experienced intense fear, helplessness or horror*, at least some of the time during the event (DSM-IV, 1994).

In the example above, both Francine and Jim experienced an event that could be categorized as a trauma. They had a road traffic accident, which could potentially have led to death and/or serious injury. Francine's response was one of intense fear and horror (upon realizing that they could not avoid the crash). She also felt very helpless as there was nothing that she or Jim could do to prevent the accident from happening.

For the purposes of this book, Francine's and Jim's story ends there. In reality, however, the subsequent rescue operation, the nature of the injuries and the experiences in hospital, the reactions of family, friends and professionals, and possibly the resulting legal proceedings could have been further sources of traumatization. *Sometimes the after-effects of a trauma can even be experienced as more traumatic than the initial traumatic event itself,* for example if a person suffers serious injuries, which require one or more painful and life-threatening operations. In addition, other people's unhelpful responses after a traumatic event can sometimes be further sources of traumatization – if others cast blame on the person or if there is an expectation that they should recover from an event far quicker than they are actually able to.

Different Types of Traumatic Events

There are many different types of traumatic events. Some of these, like road traffic accidents, are called *traumatic incidents*. Larger scale events are often called *disasters* and these can be divided into three categories: man-made disasters, natural disasters and acts of violence, crime or terrorism (Hodgkinson & Stewart, 1991). Man-made disasters imply that the trauma had occurred because of a human error or an error made by a machine or a system, designed by humans. Some examples of man-made disasters include:

- Transport disasters, by train, coach, underground or subway, such as the Intercity Express train crash in Lower Saxony, Germany in 1998;
- Air disasters, such as the Swiss Air crash near Halifax in Nova Scotia in 1998;
- Maritime disasters, such as the Zeebrugge ferry sinking in 1987;
- Fires and gas explosions;
- Severe electric shocks, caused by accidents on electric powerlines;
- Building or other structural collapses, such as the mining tragedy in Austria in 1998;
- Environmental disasters, like the nuclear catastrophe in Chernobyl in Russia in 1986.

Natural disasters constitute another category of trauma, and examples of this include:

- Earthquakes, such as the one that occurred near the port city of Kobe in Japan in 1995;
- Floods, such as those in Bangladesh in 1998;
- Hurricanes, like Hurricane Mitch in Honduras and Nicaragua in 1998;
- Forest fires, such as those in Florida in 1998;
- Volcano eruptions, avalanches.

The third category of trauma refers to acts of violence, crime and terrorism:

- Acts of domestic violence, such as physical assault;
- Stabbings;
- Hold-ups and robberies;
- Shootings, for example, at the Dunblane Primary School in Scotland in 1996 or at the high school in Denver, Colorado, in 1999;

- Bomb explosions, such as the Victoria Station bombing in London in 1991 or the nail bomb in Soho, London, in 1999;
- Rape;
- Sexual abuse;
- Acts of inhumanity, such as torture and/or solitary confinement;
- Hostage-takings;
- Wars, such as the Gulf War in 1990–1 or the war in the Balkans which started in 1995.

Man-made disasters and the traumas caused by acts of violence, crime and terrorism are often harder to adjust to, and come to terms with, than natural disasters.

Other Life Events that Can be Experienced as Traumatic

Some life events, although not outside the range of typical human experience, can become so overwhelming and frightening for some people that they respond with horror or a feeling of helplessness as intense as if it was a full traumatic experience. Such events might include job loss, redundancy, the end of a long-term relationship or divorce, miscarriage, surgical operations or the death of someone close. Not everyone will experience these events as traumatic, because it always depends on the circumstances in which the events take place and the extent to which they render the person overwhelmed and helpless.

Your Experience of Trauma

Many people live through very upsetting life events or witness them happening to others. Perhaps you have, too. The following checklist (adapted from Tyler, 1998) will help you to recognize which traumas you have experienced and how they have affected you.

7

Please read every item below and check the boxes which apply to you.

> You experienced this – and it *still* feels awful for you or causes you upset or disturbance.

>> You observed it happen to others – and it *still* makes you feel awful or upset.

>>> You experienced this – but it does not feel awful or disturbing for you *now*.

A ☐ ☐ ☐ a fire, an accident or an explosion. At home or in a car or a plane, on a boat or at a factory or farm, an office or place of work, or other

B ☐ ☐ ☐ some kind of natural disaster, like a flood, earthquake, storm, hurricane or avalanche

C ☐ ☐ ☐ an attack, where you were hit, kicked, beaten, stabbed, held at gunpoint or hurt in some other (non-sexual) way by someone who was known to you

D ☐ ☐ ☐ as above, but an attack by someone you did not know

E ☐ ☐ ☐ being in a war or some other combat situation – or a disturbance like a riot

F ☐ ☐ ☐ being taken hostage or being in prison, or being a prisoner of war

G ☐ ☐ ☐ experiencing torture, either physical or psychological, while in someone else's control

H ☐ ☐ ☐ some kind of serious, life-threatening illness

I ☐ ☐ ☐ when you were *over* 16, being physically or psychologically forced, persuaded or tricked into some kind of sexual action, against your will

continued on next page

J ☐ ☐ ☐ as above, but when you were *under* 16

K ☐ ☐ ☐ the traumatic death of another person

L ☐ ☐ ☐ some other experience, not covered by the categories above (briefly describe the experience)

....

And now decide which experience bothers you most? If you checked any of the events, either in the left or the middle columns, write their code letters in the box below, in order of seriousness (worst first).

Pay specific attention to those events that still bother you and refer back to them as you work through the rest of the book.

Loosening the Grip of Trauma

To overcome the effects of trauma it is necessary to examine the experience and work to change the distressing responses produced since the event. To cope with what has happened you need to understand your reactions. This will help you to face up to memories, thoughts and feelings which may have been deeply buried in response to the trauma and may now be hindering you from getting on with your life.

Here is how Harry felt after surviving a serious house fire:

'*After I had survived the actual trauma, I thought it was all over – but it was then when it all really began. For many months I was unable to get the images from the fire out of my mind. It was as if every day parts of the trauma were happening again. I wanted to forget it, to put it behind me, to move on with my life, but it was as if the trauma wouldn't let me. Worse still, not only were my days filled with terrifying reminders of what had happened to me, but even when I tried to get some rest from it through sleep at night it wouldn't leave me. I was haunted by repeated, recurring nightmares which seemed so real that I often woke up screaming and crying, convinced it was all happening all over again. Whatever I did, it felt at the time that I just couldn't move forward but was totally trapped by the trauma. It all felt so real that I was convinced that I was going mad.'*

Harry

Many people have the same, or very similar reactions and fears as Harry. People's responses after a trauma are often so strong and overwhelming that it is quite common for them to feel that 'they are going mad' or 'losing complete control over their life'. Sometimes these thoughts can be so unbearable that people start isolating themselves from others more and more. Such reactions are common and understandable responses to trauma. *You may be relieved to hear that you are NOT alone in experiencing these feelings.* What's more, if you are experiencing such reactions you *can* be helped to heal and recover from your trauma.

Working through a trauma can take many forms. Some people are perfectly able to do this by themselves, others may benefit much more from specialist trauma therapy. There are no hard and fast rules. What works best for one person may not work for another. The one factor that is common to all recovery from trauma is that, as you start to regain control, the trauma will gradually loosen its grip.

Harry sought out specialist trauma therapy and describes here his process of recovery.

At the beginning of the process:

'It was as if the trauma had made me fall into a very deep, waterless well. It felt very dark and lonely while I was down there and it took me a long time before I developed the courage to start climbing up its sides to get out of it. When I first started the climb I felt that I had no knowledge of what was waiting for me at the top. The higher I was able to climb, the more I

feared that something at the top might make me fall down to the bottom again. It was as if I had lost all trust in my ability to cope with what was out there for me in the world. Sometimes, this fear even made me want to climb back towards the bottom of the well again. This was because I knew that if it came to another fall it would not be quite so deep to go down. At the same time I knew that I had to continue the climb up, because the thought of staying at the bottom of this well and continuing my life in the grip of the trauma, as it had been, was unbearable.'

As Harry progressed in his recovery, the images started to change:

It felt as if I was now a fair way up from the bottom of this well. I had come to a kind of resting place, from where, for the first time, since the trauma I could gather some strength again. From here I could start to see the sky above me and there were even days when I saw some brightness and could feel the pleasant warmth from the rays of the sun. I knew that this gave me the strength to continue with the climb out of this well. I still didn't really know what was waiting for me out there once I reached the top of this well. I imagined that it might be like a huge roundabout with several roads radiating from it. At this stage I was unsure which one of these would be the "right one" for me to take.'

Still further on in his process of recovery, Harry described:

I am now sitting on the outside edge of the well and the choice of roads available for me outside the well are only three. It does not feel as overwhelming as I thought it would be. I am now starting to feel confident enough to explore and travel along one of these roads. Before doing this, however, I had decided to cover up the well. I felt I had come out of it and I now felt strong enough to live outside the well. I knew I was traveling along a totally different road compared to the one I had traveled on before the trauma. This was because the trauma had changed me, but this was not a negative change. In many ways, it felt better. I found that I had become a much more understanding and tolerant person. I had stopped taking life for

*granted, my life seemed much more meaningful and of value
to me now. I will never forget the trauma, but it no longer hurts
me to think about it nor does it occupy my daily life. Sometimes, I even feel that, however awful it was at the time, in the
end it helped me to find a different and better meaning for my
life.'*

Harry recovered from his trauma. The process of achieving this
took him over a year.

The Aim of this Book

This book is written for people (and those close to them or caring for them) who feel they are in the grip of a trauma. You
might be at different stages in the process of climbing out of
this 'deep, waterless well', as Harry described it. You might be at
the stage where you still feel very much stuck at the bottom,
where it feels dark, lonely and isolated. Or you might have started
your process of recovery and are already climbing up inside this
well.

You might not even be part of this process at all, but instead
are having to witness how a relative or somebody you care for is
struggling to find their way out of the well. You may be able to
offer a helping hand or you may feel quite powerless.

Whatever your stage or your role along the path to recovery,
Harry's example illustrates that recovery from trauma takes time
and can be a long and painful process, during which time it
can often feel that there is more darkness than light.

This book is intended as a guide to help you understand the
range of reactions, thoughts and feelings that you may be experiencing, so that you will be able to find the confidence and
courage within yourself to start or continue the difficult climb
upwards. It demonstrates, with practical advice and tested exercises, how to find new, effective ways of coping with, and finally
overcoming, traumatic stress. *This book is not intended as a
replacement for therapy, and may even encourage you to seek out
some specialist help* (see Chapter 14 where seeking professional

help is discussed in further detail). At the end of the book you will find some useful addresses or organizations, should you wish to contact a therapist.

How to Use this Book

Tips for Easy Reading

Reading a book is not the easiest task while you are in the midst of dealing with your trauma. Your levels of concentration may be poor and you may find it hard to stick with the book for very long. As this book contains a lot of information, here are some tips on how to get the most out of it:

- Don't read the book from beginning to end if that is difficult for you. Skim and browse through the book to get to know its format and content. You might find that dipping in and reading little chunks at a time is easier for you. Every person is different, and it is important that you find your own way of making the book useful to you.
- Then, if you feel up to it, read some of those passages that particularly caught your attention. Some might seem more relevant to your situation than others. Put the book down somewhere in the house where you can pick it up easily during the day to read a little bit.
- Some people find it helpful to mark or write in their books. Maybe mark those sections that are particularly relevant or helpful to you. Have the book at your side while you try out some of the practical exercises that are described.
- Try buying yourself little index cards and write down points from the book that might be useful or meaningful to you on each card. Then carry the cards around with you so that you can refer to them whenever you want to.
- You might find that parts of the book that remind you of your own experiences are rather distressing. If you feel upset, try not to worry about this, because it is quite normal and can even be part of the healing process. You might find it helps to write down your feelings or talk to someone close to you about

them. *But if your feelings are overwhelmingly strong, please have a look at the **Cautions** section below.*

- If reading seems very daunting because you have never been a good reader, or you are in the early stages of your recovery, you could ask someone close to you to read the book to you. Sometimes, it can also be very helpful to work together with a close and trusted person when you are doing the exercises from the book.

- Do not read the book last thing at night or in bed. That time should be reserved for relaxation and winding down and is not the right time to read or think about traumatic events.

Cautions

If you experience any of the following responses, please put the book aside and try to do something completely different to distract yourself:

- Feeling that you are losing touch with reality, for example, sudden extreme and overwhelming memories of the traumatic event, flashbacks or hallucinations.
- Very strong anxiety reactions, such as hyperventilation or panic attacks, an irregular heartbeat. But do remember, *some* anxiety is normal!
- Very strong physical reactions, such as trembling, feelings of extreme coldness or very hot flushes.
- Suicidal feelings.
- Feeling you want to harm yourself or others around you.
- Feelings of uncontrollable anger or rage.

If you do experience any of these responses while you are reading the book, and they don't seem to subside fairly easily after you have stopped reading, you should get in touch with your medical practitioner or therapist before continuing with it. The chapters in Part Two provide you with many tips on control strategies which you might find helpful to look at.

2

Understanding Your Reactions

Common Reactions after Trauma

The focus of this book, and of this chapter in particular, is on *your reactions* to trauma – the disturbing and frequently overwhelming feelings and symptoms that occur in the aftermath of a terrible event.

Understanding your reactions will help to reduce your sense of isolation, of being alone with your experience. You are not alone! Current research data suggests that, over the course of a lifetime, as many as 25 percent of people exposed to any type of catastrophic and highly stressful event will develop reactions that can be classified as Post-Traumatic Stress Disorder (Green, 1994). The percentage is higher still for rape and assault victims, combat veterans and those who have directly experienced community disasters.

When you are traumatized by a life event, your feelings of extreme fear, horror or helplessness can sometimes lead to a pattern of reactions which is constantly repeated and can be very disruptive to your everyday life. This, in turn, affects your ability to cope and function so that at times you may even wonder if you are losing your mind.

Reactions following trauma can be divided into three main symptom groups:

> **1 Re-experiencing the event (Intrusive reactions)**
> A feeling that you are experiencing the original event all over again, through memories intruding into your waking or sleeping life.
>
> _right *continued on next page*

15

2 Arousal reactions

You feel persistently aroused in a nervous, agitated sense, anxious, tense, unable to settle or concentrate, over-reacting very sharply to small things and, especially, have trouble sleeping.

3 Avoidance reactions

You make frantic efforts to avoid anything that could remind you of the trauma, or cause you to think or talk about it in any way. You may shut down your feelings about other people and things you normally care about and keep to yourself. You may feel unusually withdrawn and emotionally numb.

(DSM IV, 1994)

While it is likely that many of these responses will be present immediately following a traumatic incident, for most people they usually subside during the next few days or weeks. If your reactions don't subside, but instead recur over and over again, you may begin to despair that you will never be like your old self again. Your thought patterns, your attitude toward yourself begins to shift as well – you might begin to believe that you have been permanently changed or damaged. You tell yourself that you *should* be coping more efficiently. You might be bothered by feelings of shame or guilt or extreme grief.

People close to you may be expecting you to get back to normal fairly quickly, and may pressure you with statements like: 'You've changed!' or 'You're not the person you were before!'. While they may mean well, these statements serve to underscore your sense of feeling different and helpless. You may react by being snappy and irritable, very jumpy and easily startled (even by the smallest unexpected noises) or secretive and closed off. Or you might just keep it all to yourself, refusing to talk things over and avoiding friends or social gatherings.

The important thing to remember is that the very fact that these are unusual responses for you and an extreme change from your earlier personality or style of being suggests that they are indications of a *traumatic stress reaction*. Even if you are not experiencing all the symptoms mentioned here, you will recognize some and you may find that your own responses 'cluster' in certain areas. The intensity of your symptoms, the severity of interference to your normal functioning and the duration of your reactions will help you and your medical practitioner determine if further professional treatment is needed.

It is important that you begin to understand what is happening to you, and that you resolve to get whatever help is needed to assist you in becoming yourself again.

Understanding Your Symptoms

It is useful to try to understand how your body responds to stress. Recognizing that your symptoms are continuing reactions to the overpowering stress you have experienced, and therefore quite normal, is the first step in containing them and feeling more in control.

Stress was defined by Hans Selye in 1946 as a demand on the human system – mental, physical or emotional. According to this model, overwhelming traumatic stress would be perceived as an extreme demand, a threat to existence, to which the body responds by automatically mobilizing *all* its coping mechanisms to provide the necessary energy for survival – the *fight*, *flight* or *freeze* reactions. What actually happens is that massive amounts of the hormone adrenaline and other internal chemicals are produced by the body and circulated to the muscles, enabling the body to move more quickly, be stronger and more tolerant to pain. The breathing changes, the muscles are tense in anticipation of action and all the physical reactions are swift.

Post-Traumatic Stress Reactions of high arousal have sometimes been described as 'the system getting stuck on red alert' – the emergency response fails to shut off and the body is prone to surges of adrenaline, which send messages to the brain to the effect that everything in the environment continues to be dangerous and potentially threatening – just as the trauma was. In other words, traumatized individuals 'over-react' to everything. The smallest reminder of something remotely associated with the event (a slight sound, a flash of color, a smell) can set off a dramatic response. For example, a car backfires or there is a loud 'bang' in the street, etc. and you find yourself diving to the floor without thinking, as if your body has been 'programed' to expect danger and to react to the slightest diversion from the ordinary as if it were life-threatening. Such behavior could also be triggered by memory flashbacks to the actual traumatic event, or the experience of a 'replay' of all or part of the trauma before your eyes.

What seems so real to the post-trauma sufferer may not be at all apparent to companions or onlookers. It is disconcerting, and at times embarrassing, when these dramatic over-reactions occur in public or even in front of the family. Diving under a table in a restaurant in response to a dish being dropped and smashing behind you is hard to explain, even to close friends. As a result, you may become very anxious about being in public, or in social gatherings where you feel 'exposed'. You may begin to avoid such situations or to feel panicky if they are unavoidable. Your ability to predict how you will react decreases and your confidence in your coping ability suffers as a result.

In your attempts to avoid anything that would remind you of your trauma, you might have stopped listening to the television news, reading newspapers, going to familiar places or, especially, you might have stopped talking about how you feel. Even though research has shown that repeating the trauma story and acknowledging thoughts and feelings can be the most helpful healing strategy, many trauma sufferers never admit to anyone how their experience has affected them. Instead they avoid facing what they have experienced by shutting down emotionally and constructing barriers around their feelings. Detaching yourself from your feelings and from other people may be an unconscious, even automatic emotional response. It may seem to you as if there is no hope for the future, that things will never be different, so you begin to 'go through the motions' of existing in the present, without really feeling connected or engaged in it.

It should gradually be becoming clear that the symptoms of post-traumatic stress reactions can interact with each other in a kind of 'vicious circle' of responses which keep the cycle going.

Understanding Specific Reactions

It is unlikely (but not impossible) that you will have experienced *all* of the reactions discussed, so it might be helpful to pay particular attention to the ones that are the worst for you, and bother you the most frequently.

A. Re-Experiencing the Event (Intrusive Reactions)

Flashbacks

Flashbacks are *intrusive memories* that are experienced *as if the event was happening all over again*. They can occur during waking hours or be experienced as dreams or nightmares during sleep. Whether waking or sleeping, flashbacks can be extremely disturbing to the individual (and often to the family) because all the physical sensations that were present during the original trauma are usually experienced again. It is quite natural to feel that you are losing control or that your mind is being 'taken over' by past events. For seconds or minutes you may feel that you are again seeing, feeling, smelling, hearing, sensing and reacting to the event. The fear, the horror or the helplessness is also experienced again. One trauma researcher, Bessel van der Kolk (1994), has suggested that 'the body knows the score', in other words, the body retains memories that the mind is not yet ready or able to process. The traumatic images or pictures are presented again and again, as the mind struggles to make sense of what has happened.

Intrusive Recollections

While not every vivid memory is experienced as a flashback, most people will have trouble switching off their recollection of a traumatic event. Very simple things in daily life (even breathing heavily after hurrying or being pushed in a crowd) can become triggers that set off a whole chain of traumatic associations in an instant. This can often happen without you even being aware of the initial connection or trigger at the beginning of the chain. Be assured these are not signs that you are losing your mind! It shows that the mind is struggling to use its cognitive processes to make sense of what has happened to the world you knew *before* the trauma. Your sense of how the world *should be* has been violated. It feels as if the 'bubble of safety' that surrounded you before the trauma, and made it possible for you to get through the day, has now burst. Therefore, the world no longer feels safe and secure.

> *'I had been the victim of an armed robbery. In order not to be harmed I handed the money over to the robber. For weeks after the trauma I could not forget what had happened. I could not stop myself from thinking about parts of the event, which seemed to pop into my mind at the most unexpected times. I could still remember every little thing in detail. It was like a film being replayed over and over again. I also found myself feeling all the reactions that I had had during this event and sometimes it felt as if it were happening all over again. I re-experienced the shivering that I had felt, the horror and helplessness and I even felt the anger that I had felt when the robber ran away after having kicked an innocent customer to the ground. All this was extremely distressing to me. It felt so out of control, as I could never predict when these reactions would overtake me again.'*
>
> Ray

B. Arousal Reactions

Sleep Disturbance

When you are highly agitated, unable to relax and constantly on the alert for danger, it is, of course, very difficult to enjoy restful sleep. In fact, disturbed sleep is the after-effect most commonly reported by people who have experienced traumas (Woodward, 1993) and this may manifest itself in several ways: finding it very difficult to settle to sleep, waking in the middle of the night, drenched in sweat, having nightmares or recurring dreams, restless sleep with limbs moving, crying out in sleep, waking in the early morning, e.g. 4 or 5 a.m., and finding it difficult to fall back to sleep again.

'I was a pilot and twenty-six years old when one of the engines on my plane caught fire during a military air display. I was able to land the plane and was pulled out by a ground crew together with my co-pilot just before the plane exploded into a fireball a few seconds later. Immediately after the trauma, I could not stop myself from sleeping. I felt tired and slept many hours – it was almost like being in a coma. Then, about four days after the trauma, exactly the opposite happened. I lay awake in bed for hours and could not settle to sleep. When I eventually did get off to sleep I had the most horrific dreams and kept waking up in cold sweat and terror, finding it impossible to get back to sleep. I could count myself lucky if I got more than four hours sleep a night. I also became terribly irritable and found it hard to control sudden rushes of anger that kept welling up in me without any apparent reason. I could blow up over the smallest things, such as someone forgetting to close a door. After a while my friends stopped saying certain things to me and started behaving very cautiously around me. This made me feel even angrier and I became bitter and resentful towards them. Inside myself I had lost all my previous confidence and I felt very insecure about my indecisiveness, my constant fear of danger and my complete inability to take things in around me. People often had to repeat themselves several times before I could register what they were saying. I also had totally lost my ability to remember dates and appointments and found it impossible to concentrate on reading for much longer than 10 minutes.'

Peter

Bad Temper and Lack of Concentration

All the jumpiness and increased sensitivity is bound to have an impact on a person's mood, temper and ability to concentrate on everyday tasks. You might find yourself becoming very negative, argumentative or easily irritated, in ways that were very unlike you before the traumatic event. You could be angry with yourself for not being able to 'snap out of it'. Or you might find yourself shouting at co-workers or family members about trivial things or because they are pressing you to make simple decisions you don't feel ready or able to make. Such irritation could escalate if you feel that you have suffered because of government bureaucracy, the legal system or institutional mishandling. Often that deep-seated anger will show itself in biting sarcasm or in attempts to over-control every situation, because inside you are conscious of how difficult it is for you to concentrate and attend to details and you deeply fear making mistakes.

Hyper-Alertness and Exaggerated Concern for Safety

If the trauma you experienced was sudden and dramatic it is quite natural that your previous sense of safety and your ability to handle situations will have been utterly shaken. You may now be especially watchful of your environment. You may be checking things or places for safety and see potential danger in ordinary situations. This could include being especially careful about where you choose to sit when going out, for example, considering certain seats, such as the one with its back to the window, as unsafe domain. This concern might also extend to other people around you and to them you may come across as 'over-controlling' in your attempts to ensure their safety. This feeling of being on 'red alert' – assessing potential danger all the time – can be extremely draining as your senses have to work overtime to achieve this high level of security.

Exaggerated Startle Response and Panic Attacks

Sudden noises and unexpected movements can startle you severely and the physical arousal reactions that go with this can stay with you for a long time, making you feel nervous and on edge. Nervous agitation might also be experienced as shakiness, light-headedness or even lead to a full-blown panic attack. Panic attacks can occur out of the blue, seemingly without warning, and are quite terrifying. They produce physical symptoms like sudden shortness of breath, severe chest pains or a feeling of dizziness or faintness. A panic attack is another way of showing, in an extreme fashion, the result of (traumatic) stress overload. Quite frequently, it is difficult to pinpoint a direct cause and some people suffer panic attacks *after* the trauma has passed. But the occurrence of such panic attacks may signal that there are still some deeper feelings to be dealt with. Understanding that they are a sign to 'pay more attention to yourself and your healing' and *not* the onset of a disabling disease, will make them less frightening. Use the strategies in the chapters on 'Managing Reactions' to help you to gain confidence and worry less about panic reactions.

C. Avoidance and Emotional Numbing Reactions

'Avoidance' reactions can manifest themselves in several ways:

Avoidance Behavior

Avoidance behavior means avoiding or literally keeping out of the way of *any* person, place or thing that might be a reminder (even very remotely) of the trauma. In particular, avoiding things that have already served as reminders or 'triggers' and caused great anxiety or other overwhelming feelings, such as rage, sadness, guilt or disabling grief, or that have set off a flashback. Thus your world gets narrower and narrower. Frequently, you don't want to 'lose face' by admitting that you are avoiding anything, so you make up excuses or make elaborate arrangements to avoid encountering the site of the trauma – the building, place, person or activity (such as driving after a road traffic accident).

Emotional Numbness

A form of avoidance behavior that is much less easy to identify and understand is emotional numbness – a feeling of hollowness or of being in a void. The traumatized person may feel as though a part of them (the feeling part) has been removed or has died and they experience a sense of being shut down, without the capacity to connect to the world through feelings. This can affect your capacity to laugh, to feel happy or even your ability to cry although you may still feel very sad. Sometimes you might feel that even your capacity to love has been affected, and this can be very frightening, especially if, as a parent, you feel that your capacity to love and feel for your children has dried up.

Alienation, Disconnection and Difficulty with Intimacy

A third form of avoidance is the difficulty in getting close to and communicating with other people. Often people experiencing this feel that they have lost the capacity to connect to the world and their loved ones. They feel a pressure from friends and loved ones to become the person they were before the trauma, but this may not be possible. The response to the pressure to be 'normal' may be to withdraw from company and say very little and there might even be resentment toward people who expect you to 'get over it'. Another common experience is to feel disengaged from other people in your surroundings, as if you are watching things from behind a glass window. You might even feel, for short periods of time, as though you are observing yourself from outside your body.

Your sense of touch and ability to cope with intimacy and physical contact may be affected, too. If you jump when others touch you unexpectedly and shy away from hugging or displays of affection, this is probably because you are so caught up in trying to keep yourself together and contain your feelings that you can't respond to unexpected demands. If, at times, your guard is lowered (for example, during sex or when falling asleep) this may provoke feelings of sudden panic. The reason for this is that reverting to your former ways of feeling will also 'get you closer' to the traumatic experience and the possibility of having to go through it all again.

Alcohol, Drugs and Comfort Eating

People will often use alcohol or drugs to escape or block out the painful reactions connected to their trauma and obtain a temporary respite. You might dread falling asleep, because of disturbing or repetitive dreams or fear 'losing control' by letting down your guard and becoming too relaxed. When one's sleep is disturbed over a long period, there is a strong temptation to take a pill to enhance sleep.

Some people also use food and comfort eating as a way of blocking out painful feelings temporarily. For some, just the action of filling themselves with food can alleviate feelings of inner emptiness and unconnectedness.

Although such behavior can temporarily improve things, the improvement is artificial and can have a rebound effect. Over-use of alcohol, drugs, comfort eating or any other artificially induced 'numbing' agent can actually inhibit restful sleep and simply compound the problem.

Avoidance behavior or emotional numbing reactions are often motivated by the desire to prevent further pain and to protect the wounded self through a very narrow interpretation of what is 'safe'. A number of factors such as guilt or self-blame or a particularly horrible detail which you are keeping secret may increase the pressure to preserve that 'numbness' as it seems safer. Again, the end result can be counter-productive and you may end up isolated and prevented from moving on with your life and your healing.

'Until my rape at the age of twenty, I had been very sociable, outgoing and perfectly happy with my life. I had several close girlfriends and had good relationships with men. I had enjoyed myself at a friend's party and had trusted Mathew who was well known in the local community to take me home. On our way home we bumped into three of Mathew's friends whom I had never met before. It was then that Mathew's behavior started to change. At first I thought that maybe I was a bit too sensitive, especially as I had drunk a bit at the party. However, slowly I became frightened by the change in Mathew's tone of voice. Cheered on by these friends, he started to become really verbally abusive towards me, calling me names that nobody had ever dared to call me before. We were still several minutes walk away from my home, in a very rural area, when Mathew pushed me to the ground and raped me in front of his friends, who shouted obscene words at me. I was completely frozen and so shocked that I was unable to shout or defend myself in any way.

I felt totally numb when I eventually found my way home. Although I love my parents, they are elderly and a little old-fashioned in their views and I felt I could not confide in them. I also feared that nobody would believe me anyway if I accused

Mathew, who was well respected in the community, of having raped me in front of his friends. I felt that people might either laugh at me and not take me seriously or accuse me of having led Mathew on at the party. I felt ashamed and dirty at that thought and I blamed myself and felt guilty for not having been stronger and stood up to Mathew and his friends.

I kept my secret for eight years, until therapy finally enabled me to work things through. Over these years, I changed completely. I broke off all contact with my previous friends and apart from going to work I was spending all my evenings at home. I never went to a party again or any other social events after the rape. When people invited me I would make up excuses about being too busy with other things. Eventually, all invitations stopped. I was unable to use any public transport and only felt safe going out during the light hours. In the winter months, when I had to return from work in the dark, I would park my car right outside the office block and at the other end drive up almost to my front door. I was dutiful at work but withdrew whenever any of my colleagues tried to get close to me. Emotionally I felt completely empty and I couldn't experience any loving feelings any longer, not even really towards my parents. They were worried about the change in my personality but couldn't help, as they did not understand my reasons for behaving in the way I did. Occasionally, if my sleeping was very badly affected by intrusive memories I would use alcohol to help me relax and settle to sleep more easily. Eventually I started drinking a bit too much. Although my world felt fairly safe and under my control, I was very isolated, cut-off and lonely.'

Cathy

D. Other Reactions Following Trauma

Depression and Traumatic Grief

In the early stages, following a traumatic incident, some people want to sleep all the time. This is a common immediate reaction, but if it continues for months it may signal the presence of depression.

Depression literally means 'pressed down'. It is very common for those who are grieving to go through a stage of depression. The burden of overwhelming sadness that accompanies a severe loss can be too much for some survivors to bear. They find it almost impossible to imagine life carrying on without the loved one they have lost and feel lost and helpless themselves.

Loss of a limb or limbs, or the loss of former looks through physical disfigurement, can be just as painful as losing another person through death. It can feel as if a part of yourself has died. And often, less obvious losses, such as being made redundant, losing friends and associates, a miscarriage (or therapeutic abortion), loss of physical strength or ability – or loss of faith in yourself – can be the trigger for depressed feelings. You might begin to think 'I'll *never* get beyond this' or 'I'll always feel this way' and you might minimize any efforts you have made on your own behalf. As you sink further into depression, your thinking becomes more negative and may focus on feelings of worthlessness. Self-defeating thoughts, such as: 'I've never been any good', 'I always screw things up', may become familiar patterns in your thinking. There may even be a slightly superstitious tendency in your thinking: 'Bad things happen to anyone who's around me', 'I should have expected something like this. Things were going just too well for me.'

Depressed thinking is so caught up in negative patterns that it becomes difficult to concentrate on other things. Your mind may feel as if it is racing and at the same time you experience overwhelming fatigue. Some people feel little motivation to eat, and over longer periods of time this can lead to significant weight loss, even health problems. Alternatively, others might use comfort eating to block out their distress. Memory for everyday details, appointments and even ordinary, routine activities is likely to be unreliable. The term 'burn-out' is often used to describe the experience of those who have been doing too much for too long, trying to cope with impossible demands and finally sink into a state of exhaustion. Burn-out can also be applied to people who have been trying very hard to cope after trauma, doing all the 'right things' and yet still find themselves sinking more and more into a depression.

'I was a warehouse controller when I lost my right eye in an industrial accident. One of the sprung metal fittings on a piece of machinery had come undone through my own doing and hit my head, damaging my right eye. After the initial shock and a short period of hospitalization, my company offered me a different job on the factory floor, which I could do with the functioning of one eye only. I tried to get on with life and continue with my work as best as I could. The accident was never really talked about anymore. I tried to ignore my internal emotional reactions, because I was so ashamed of them. I felt that I should be brave, after all, accidents happen all the time in life and, if anything, this accident had been caused by my own wrong-doing. I shouldn't have fiddled with the machine when I did. However, I was unable to get rid of my feelings and I noticed myself becoming more and more depressed about the loss of my right eye. I blamed myself and I didn't feel like a proper man anymore. I noticed people staring at me sometimes as if I was some kind of alien. I often felt like screaming out at them, but then I would tell myself that: "It had been my own fault … that I only got what I deserved … and that I shouldn't be so stupid now and pull myself together!" I felt very down and upset, but also very alone because I felt too ashamed to talk about my feelings with anybody.'

Bob

Guilt and self-blame

It is very common for people to blame themselves for all or parts of the traumatic incident. They might think that if only they had done things differently on the day of the trauma, it might never have happened. Often they take personal responsibility for the terrible outcomes, thinking that they 'should have known' and thus could have made their decisions differently before or during the trauma. They might also feel guilt for having survived when others didn't. A belief that 'It should have been me who died. Her life was worth so much more than mine', is typical of survivor guilt.

Decreased self-esteem and loss of confidence

As we have seen, one feature of self-blame is a very negative pattern of thinking, where you constantly put yourself down and take no credit for those things that you have achieved. Gradually, your confidence is eroded, leading to feelings of worthlessness and very low self-esteem, which may be further confirmed by the disabling effects of other reactions to the trauma. For example, you may not understand your reactions to the trauma and may belittle yourself for withdrawing from people or avoiding activities that previously you would have really liked to do. Negative thoughts lead to a sense that you are losing control, and even losing your mind: you are caught in the downward spiral of low self-esteem.

> '*I had been a dentist, but had to give this up as a result of the severe back injuries that I sustained during a climbing excursion, when I slipped and fell, before the rope had been securely fastened by one of the fellow climbers. I had difficulties finding a suitable alternative job. Although I got some offers of work, I usually didn't last very long in the positions I started in, because of the disabling chronic pain, which would keep me off work for long periods of time. I lost all my confidence. I withdrew more and more from my previous circle of friends, because they were all so successful in their careers and I felt ashamed and embarrassed at not being able to keep up with them. I felt useless and hopeless about myself and about my abilities and prospects in my future life.*'

> *Pam*

What is Post-Traumatic Stress Disorder (PTSD)?

You may have been told by your doctor, psychiatrist, clinical psychologist or any other mental health care professional, that you are suffering from Post-Traumatic Stress Disorder, or PTSD for short.

Post-Traumatic Stress Disorder is the term given to a particular range and combination of reactions following a trauma. It conveys to a health care professional which reactions you may be experiencing and how best to help you. If you continue to experience the responses described in the previous section for longer than a month, it is likely that your reactions will be classed as Post-Traumatic Stress Disorder. This diagnosis will also depend on how many reactions you are experiencing in each of the three symptom groups and how frequent, severe and disabling they are to you.

Whether you have full-blown Post-Traumatic Stress Disorder or suffer from Post-Traumatic Stress Reactions, the content of this book will be equally relevant to you. As a general rule, the sooner you start working through the effects of the trauma and the more you understand what is happening to you, the better equipped you will be to take control of your recovery process.

3

Understanding the Reactions of Families and Loved Ones

Carrying the Emotional Scars of Trauma

'The trauma seems to have changed him! He is no longer the person I used to love'

This statement was made by Lucy, the wife of Phil, survivor of a commuter train crash.

'Phil used to be so loving and caring. When he came home from work he would cuddle me and ask me if I had had a good day. We would typically sit and have a drink together and share each other's experiences from the day. We would often go out, meet friends, entertain at home. We would laugh and joke together and there was a lot of intimacy, closeness and a very warm atmosphere between the two of us. This has now completely changed! Phil hardly greets me now when he gets home from work. Usually he goes straight upstairs into his study, where he will just sit in his chair, sometimes just staring into space. At other times he reads the newspaper, but I have the feeling that he doesn't actually take in what he reads, because it seems to take him hours to turn a few pages. I no longer look forward to Phil coming home – the worst is his temper. He gets so angry and shouts about such unimportant, petty things. The other day, I hadn't completely turned off a tap in the bathroom, so that it was still dripping a little. Rather than going to turn it off, which Phil would have done in the past, he really had a go at me. He ranted and raved, I was so frightened that

31

I thought he might even hit me. We also hardly ever go out now. Friends have given up calling on us. On the few occasions that they do come round, Phil is not really entertaining anymore. It is as if he has lost all his sense of fun – he takes everything that others say so seriously. He has also become so controlling; he has to check on every little thing to ensure it's safe. He doesn't seem to trust me anymore and will check on things, for example, that the gas is turned off, even when I have assured him that I have done it already. Sometimes he really gets on my nerves with his behavior.'

Lucy

Lucy is not alone in feeling this way. Many partners of trauma survivors and other members of the trauma victim's family find it difficult to cope with the emotional scars left by the trauma on their loved ones. After an initial period of relief, partners and family often feel increasingly puzzled, confused and helpless as they begin to witness the emotional and psychological changes incurred by the trauma, often long after the physical wounds have healed. Most partners or family members try to help the trauma survivors as best as they can, but it is often very difficult for the recipients to receive this help and for it to have any effect.

The Ripple Effect or How Trauma Affects Family and Loved Ones

The effects of trauma are felt in families, partnerships and in any other relationships that the trauma survivors have. Unfortunately, the ripple effect of the trauma on close relationships is often ignored and not addressed by professionals, whose main concern is to aid the trauma survivors.

Trauma can have devastating long-term consequences on relationships. It is not uncommon for previously well-functioning marriages or partnerships to break up and for family members to become increasingly alienated from each other. The resulting effects of these break-ups or breakdowns can then lead to further, so-called secondary traumatization. The trauma survivor can thus end up in a downward spiral that seems to make the prospect of recovery more and more remote.

In order to lessen the destructive impact of the ripple effect it is important to understand the nature of the emotional scarring that the trauma survivor bears and the effect that this can have on previously normal, well-functioning relationships.

The Need for Closeness and Intimacy

As Lucy described in the example above, one of the former positive features of her marriage with Phil was the degree of intimacy and warmth between them. Closeness and intimacy are key requirements for a well-functioning human relationship. *Unfortunately, survivors of trauma often lose their capacity for such closeness after their experience.*

> 'I had been so happy with my wife Paula, before the trauma. Afterwards, there were no real reasons at all why I shouldn't still be as happy, or maybe even happier than before – because I had actually survived the trauma. I knew in my head that in many ways I should appreciate my relationship with Paula even more now. She was so good to me, trying to help me as best as she could, trying to be supportive. However, it was as if something inside me had been switched off by the trauma. This was my capacity to feel. I felt completely dead inside, even though there was absolutely no external reason for me to be this way. I felt so out of control and so helpless. I wanted to find this internal switch, but nothing that I tried seemed to be able to help me to get back my feelings. I noticed how Paula suffered from the distance between us and the internal loneliness that she felt as a result, but I myself felt frozen like a stone, unable to move closer towards her.'
>
> Mark

Mark's description captures very well how many people feel after a trauma: an internal deadness, a feeling of helplessness to change or do anything about it. The feeling of emotional deadness often interferes with the need for closeness in a relationship and can also have a profound effect on a couple's ability to have intimate sexual contact. There can be both a loss of capacity for emotional closeness as well as for physical intimacy. Sometimes it is hard for a traumatized person to tolerate touch. Partners can jump to the conclusion that their loved ones don't love them anymore and members of the family can also feel rejected. The result is often further distancing, as partners and family members tend to give up after a period of being locked out of their loved one's internal, emotional world. Nevertheless, as Mark's example illustrates, this is usually the last thing that a trauma survivor actually wants, nor is it helpful for the process of recovery.

Remember these are feelings that a trauma survivor can't avoid; they are the direct result of the emotionally scarring effects of trauma. It is usually not the case that trauma survivors cease to love the people who were close to them before the trauma, but rather that, for the present, they can't respond to those people normally, because they have lost access to their capacity to love.

The Need for Openness and Communication

Well-functioning relationships need openness and good communication to thrive. In order to feel connected to another person it is essential to talk openly. Again, such a facility is frequently blocked as a result of the trauma.

'Before the trauma I used to share everything with Kim. We would sit for hours in the evening and chat away about things. We used to plan together and shared most of our responsibilities in life – we were a great team. Since the trauma something has changed. Kim doesn't really understand how I feel. I have talked to her about the trauma in a general way, but I couldn't describe to her all the ghastly details that keep haunting me day after day. I feel embarrassed and ashamed about feeling so out of control internally, and often I feel physically sick when reminders of scenes that I witnessed during the trauma keep intruding into my mind throughout the day (and night). Any person who hasn't been through this couldn't really understand how it feels and I wouldn't want to burden Kim with the internal turmoil that I am going through. It would only worry her.

As a consequence, we don't really talk as we used to. Kim still tries, but I also find it very difficult to concentrate on her chatter – it even gets on my nerves sometimes. Kim says that I am often silent whereas in the past I would have had my say. She feels that I am not as open with her as I used to be. But how can I be?'

Steven

It is often very hard for trauma survivors to share their internal distress and their experiences with others, however close. One reason for this may be, as in Steven's example, the wish to protect the loved one and not to burden them. Another reason for Steven is that he feels embarrassed and ashamed of his feelings. People often fear that they are 'going mad' or 'losing complete control' after a trauma and they may feel that others would not really understand them, or may indeed confirm these fears.

In addition, opening up and talking about aspects of the trauma can reawaken painful memories and distressing emotions. This can be a source of worry, particularly if they don't understand their feelings and see them as a sign of personal weakness, rather than as a natural part of the healing process. A further reason can be the spoken or unspoken expectation 'that they ought to have got over things by now' which trauma survivors can pick up from others around them. Being aware of this can definitely make a person keep things to themselves. Difficulties with concentration and the ability to absorb only limited amounts of information at a time, as described by Steven above, are also common reasons for not engaging in communication.

Remember that opening up and talking often isn't easy for people who have been involved in traumas. In order to reduce the impact of the emotional scarring, try to encourage those who have been traumatized to allow themselves to open up to their loved ones.

The Need for Trust, a Sense of Predictability and Safety

Trust, a sense of predictability and security are all very important factors in healthy human relationships and social interactions. Unfortunately, it is often the very nature of trauma that shatters the capacity for trust in a traumatized person.

'My sense of trust and safety has completely gone. The world around me has become completely unpredictable and I can never relax enough to feel safe now. I notice that people in my family have become very cautious around me. They seem to avoid certain topics of conversation and seem to talk about me behind my back. I know that I often blow up at them over completely stupid things, which in the past I would only have laughed about. I hate myself for it, but don't seem to be able to control it or stop it. It is as if, suddenly, a really black cloud completely grips hold of me and installs in me this capacity to destroy everything around me. I sometimes even get a perverse sense of pleasure from this wish to destroy and dismantle. I find myself being sarcastic with people, who before the trauma I cared about very much. Also I don't trust anyone anymore. I sense danger everywhere and I find myself checking what others have done to make sure that they have done it properly.'

Will

Frequently, a traumatized person's loss of trust, and a sense of safety and predictability, is mirrored in their behavior towards those around them.

Remember that a traumatized person doesn't *want* to act in this way, but often can't help it. Their behavior reflects their magnified fears about the world after their trauma. They will need to relearn how to trust and feel safe, and the more predictable and reassuring you can be the more helpful it will be for the process of their recovery.

The Need for Fun, Leisure and Relaxation

Relationships also need to be fun and to contain space for leisure and relaxation. The impact of trauma often makes this very difficult to achieve naturally.

'Tom and I used to have great fun together. We shared similar interests and most of our evenings and weekends were spent *doing things that we both enjoyed. We were very active sports people, used to play squash, tennis and go riding together. We also used to dance and liked going to the theatre, cinema and had a lot of friends. Doing these things together created a great sense of unity and closeness in our relationship. All this is gone now. Tom doesn't really understand. He feels I ought to be happy that I survived. I could have been far worse off, my physical injuries weren't even that bad. He is right and I still can't help myself from feeling the way I do. It is as if all my motivation and interest in any activity has gone. I just can't be bothered with anything. Everything seems such an effort and I just prefer to stay at home and don't want to see anyone or do anything. Tom wants to include me in his plans for our next holiday. I used to love holidays, but even my sense of pleasure for those is now gone. I don't really feel like planning anything at the moment. All I can think about is how I can get through tomorrow – I have no sense of a future for myself.'*

Jennifer

Both interest and motivation in previously enjoyable activities can be severely impaired in people who have suffered a trauma. This can be especially difficult in families where one of the parents has been traumatized and no longer feels able to play with the children or do all the fun things that they used to do together. The lack of a sense of a future, as Jennifer described, can also be very disabling to the affected person and to others around them. It can feel as if life has completely stopped at the time of the trauma and this is often exactly how it feels to the traumatized person.

It is important to help the traumatized person slowly to find ways of re-engaging with their present life. Their lack of interest is *not* a reflection of how they feel about their partner or others close to them, but rather another outcome of the trauma.

How to Survive the Trauma Together

The emotional scars of trauma can really get in the way of previously well-functioning relationships, whether they are with partners, family, friends or even colleagues at work. It is important to recognize that the traumatized person doesn't do these things deliberately to hurt or to destroy, but that they are a true reflection of how badly they have been affected by the trauma. True healing and recovery does take time.

Here are some tips for surviving the trauma together:

- Don't pressure the traumatized person to get better, but acknowledge that they probably don't like what they are going through themselves. Allow them to heal in their own time. Only they will know how long this process will take, so be patient and work to create this time for healing with them.

- Recognize that each individual is different and accept that there is no standard way of recovering. There is no right or wrong way of responding. Traumas are bound to affect people in different ways.

- As often as possible, indicate gently to the traumatized person that you are prepared to listen to their story, if you feel able, and if they feel able to tell it. But try not to exert any pressure.

- Try to appreciate that strong emotions are likely to be in evidence when people think or talk about their trauma. When they first start talking, it may feel to them as if they are being transported back to the time of the trauma and that their emotions and physical responses might be almost as strong as at the time they originally experienced them. It is important that these feelings are expressed as part of the normal healing process.

- Maintain as much stability and routine as you can at this time. It is important that the traumatized person learns to regain a sense of safety; some anchoring might need to take place before any new life changes can be initiated. For instance, this would not be the right time to make major life decisions, such as moving house, changing jobs, etc. It is advisable to wait at least six months, if possible.

- Treat each other as equal partners. Just because a person might be suffering from disabling responses doesn't mean that they are in any way inferior to you. The more you can establish a healing partnership, the better. Ask the traumatized person for feedback on what feels helpful and what is not helpful to them when you are together.

- Read this book together. Try to establish with your partner what kind of a role you could usefully play in order to give the maximum help in the recovery process.

- Work out a contract for healing together. Write down what is blocking you in your relationship at the moment. Agree what you would like to be able to change in due course so that your relationship will be happier and more rewarding. Set down what you will do for each other and how you will work together to achieve these changes over time.

- Partners need support too. It is helpful if you find a person outside your immediate family to confide in and share your feelings with. Support services and information sessions might be available through professional agencies to partners of the traumatized. These can help you understand more about your partner's reactions and make you respond more patiently.

- Sometimes your partner's reactions can be so strong that you will feel overwhelmed and need to withdraw. In these situations it is vital to ensure that you keep safe. Afterwards, your partner will be grateful that you have protected yourself.

4

Issues For Professionals and Carers: Vicarious Traumatization

Warning: 'Trauma can be contagious!'

Working with trauma sufferers requires us to confront and cope with some of life's deepest issues. Trauma work brings us face to face with experiences that are outside most people's range of experience as well as our own. We are frequently required to test our own fundamental beliefs about the world. Trauma not only changes the people who have experienced it, it also changes the professionals and carers who are working with it.

Astonishingly, many professionals who work within this field respond to ever-increasing demands without stopping to consider the impact that this type of work might be having on them in the long term. It is a common pattern for professionals to place the least emphasis on their own care and nurturing, but in the long run this may be a false economy.

There might still be a stigma attached to admitting that, as professionals, we can also be affected by our work and the impact of the trauma we are having to deal with. Yet working with trauma does mean being faced repeatedly with the darker side of life and shouldering serious issues, often over long periods of time. Therefore, in order to be able to sustain such work over long periods of time and at the same time remain healthy and motivated, professionals and carers must learn to develop their own nurturing strategies and put in place appropriate support and back-up systems.

What is Vicarious Traumatization and Can We Avoid It?

Saakvitne and Pearlman (1996) give the following definition in their excellent book, *Transforming the Pain*: 'Vicarious or secondary traumatization is the transformation of the therapist's inner experience as a result of empathic engagement with survivor clients and their trauma material.'

Vicarious traumatization is thus the unavoidable by-product of working with trauma survivors in a caring and empathic way. It is the natural consequence of caring for and helping traumatized people and it is important not to see it as a sign of weakness.

If vicarious traumatization can't be avoided, trauma professionals and carers need to learn to accept and recognize it as an integral part of their trauma work and devise coping strategies and resources in order to sustain long-term, healthy working in this field.

How to Recognize It

Trauma work can change professionals and other carers working within this field. It can damage, unsettle or throw us off our chosen path.

'Vera was a qualified Clinical Psychologist, who had been working in the field of Adult Mental Health for five years when she started to get an increasing amount of referrals of clients who had been in traumas. For years her workload had been high generally and this did not change now. Vera tried to approach her trauma work in the same way as she had always approached her other work. She put in long hours, was a very caring and committed therapist, but the atmosphere in her department was quite anonymous, with everyone minding their own business and she had very little support from her colleagues. After a while Vera started to notice that something inside her had changed. There were times when she found herself carrying distressing, traumatizing images

in her head, which her clients had shared in the session. This did not only happen during work time but also in the evenings and at night. She felt embarrassed because she thought that as a therapist she ought to be able to handle these thoughts. She didn't really feel comfortable with her colleagues and therefore had nobody to share her concerns with. She tried to ignore them by telling herself that she should know better and that this, after all, was an unavoidable part of her work. A few months later Vera got a visit from her long-standing friend, Eva, who she had last seen a year ago. Eva suggested various outings and activities together, but Vera found herself quite switched off and couldn't summon up the energy to do very much. She felt exhausted and was unable to experience any sense of pleasure or joy in any of the things they did together. On many occasions she noticed thoughts or images relating to client material intruding into her mind. Everything else around her seemed so trivial compared to what these people had had to suffer. Eva noticed that Vera had really changed. She felt that Vera had become very cynical and that she had lost her natural enthusiasm for life The previous year she had been very active and had engaged in many activities outside work, but this year it all seemed different. Eva's feedback eventually helped Vera to look for some help and support for herself.'

Vera

As demonstrated in Vera's example above, the effect of vicarious traumatization tends to develop gradually over time and it is often easy not to notice that you are being affected by it until something happens to highlight changes in your personality and lifestyle.

Signs to watch out for:

- Reduced energy, exhaustion, lack of motivation and feeling that you have no time for yourself.
- Disconnection from others – other people don't really understand you; you don't feel close to people anymore. Difficulties with your partner or with other close relationships.

- Emotional blunting – finding it difficult to experience emotions; not being able to laugh or cry as you used to; not caring. Being less self-reflective and less able to sort out your own feelings.
- Questioning career choice, feeling ineffectual.
- Errors in maintaining professional boundaries, failure to set limits, a general sense of failure and resentment.
- Social withdrawal, loss of interest in social activities.
- Feelings of despair and hopelessness, a bleakness in your outlook.
- Feelings of weakness, shame or guilt, often because your own problems seem comparatively minor compared with those of your clients.
- Loss of belief in the justice of life or in a sense of balance between good and bad, resulting in cynicism and bitterness.
- Heightened sense of danger, feeling less secure, scanning for danger, including for violence or aggression, in your environment.
- Sleeping problems and nightmares.
- Difficulties in concentrating and making decisions; not listening to others; confusion and disturbance of organizational skills.
- Lack of self-control, increased anger, impatience, strained relationships with others.
- Loss of trust in others.
- Alterations in sensory experiences, e.g. intrusive imagery and flashbacks.

Other changes to look out for :

- Changes to your inner sense of identity and equilibrium, i.e. you find it harder to experience and integrate strong feelings or to maintain an inner sense of connection with others or to feel grounded and anchored within yourself.
- Changes to your world view and spirituality, i.e. you have lost or changed your philosophy of life, your values and beliefs about others and the external world.

If you notice any of the aforementioned changes in yourself it could be helpful to share them with another person and to identify ways in which you could reverse or control the impact of some of them. You should not feel it is a sign of weakness if you do experience any of these responses, but rather a warning that you need to do something to redress the balance in your work and life.

How to Help Yourself

It is often the case that people working as caring professionals are not very good at self-care. However, in order to be genuinely helpful to their clients they have a responsibility to take proper care of themselves. Therapists who are 'burnt out' or give their clients the impression that they shouldn't 'burden' them with their feelings because they seem too exhausted and needy themselves are not going to benefit their clients and will give a poor service.

Although, as professionals you may not be able to avoid being affected by vicarious traumatization, you can avoid being controlled or damaged by it.

In order to minimize the damaging effects of vicarious traumatization it is helpful to be aware of possible contributing factors in your environment. Generally speaking, these might include (Saakvitne and Pearlman, 1996):

- the nature of the trauma work
- the organizational context in which this work takes place
- the social and cultural context in which your work takes place
- individual factors
- professional factors.

More specifically, working with trauma can be especially difficult when:

- there is no provision for staff respite (e.g. shared coverage, adequate time off)
- staff carry unrealistically high case loads
- there is not enough adequately qualified supervision available

- the organization fails to recognize the value of trauma work or the impact that it might have on professionals
- the organization fails to work with staff to identify and address signs of vicarious traumatization
- the organization does not provide opportunities for continuing education
- holidays are inadequate
- personal therapy for therapists is not supported
- professionals also have to cope with stressful personal circumstances
- professionals feel reluctant or create obstacles to using supervision and consultation, seeking education or taking vacations
- professionals are new or under-qualified for this work
- professionals carry unrealistically high expectations of themselves as therapists.

Now you are aware of the potential risk factors, identify for yourself:

1 which of those may apply to you
2 what you could do to change them
3 how and when you will make these changes.

Assess your needs and note down how you have addressed and how you will address in the future the potential effects of stress in the table below:

Your needs:	What do you already do?	What changes would you like to make from now on?
Taking care of yourself	_____ _____ _____ _____ _____	_____ _____ _____ _____ *continued on next page*

LIBRARY, UNIVERSITY OF CHESTER

Your needs:	What do you already do?	What changes would you like to make from now on?
Nurturing activities		
Holidays and other escapes		
Creating meaning in your work and life		
Challenging negative beliefs and assumptions		
Social activities		

Take some time to work out which areas you will need to change in both your work and private life. It would be helpful to find yourself a 'working partner', maybe a professional colleague, with whom you could discuss your planned changes and monitor your progress.

Special Issues for Other Trauma Care Response Groups

Although the main focus of this chapter has been the effect of vicarious traumatization on health care professionals, trauma work can have an equally profound effect on other trauma care response groups, such as emergency and rescue services and community welfare services, humanitarian aid organizations, and other voluntary or fund-aided helpers. When people are working outside their normal range of duties, the danger of vicarious traumatization increases.

Organizations vary in the range of support they provide for their personnel but generally, the more back-up and support your organization provides for you and the more you take personal responsibility for maintaining a good balance in your life, the better shielded you are from the potentially damaging effects of trauma work.

Although dealing with traumatic events will be part of your daily experience if you work for the emergency services or for another front-line carer group, there will still be certain events that will affect you more than others. These are likely to be details of events that feel distressing to you personally or incidents that have a more disturbing impact on you and members of your colleague groups.

Critical Incident Stress Debriefing

Having recognized the potentially disturbing effect of certain traumatic events many human service organizations now use a procedure called Critical Incident Stress Debriefing (CISD) to help their staff cope better with especially traumatizing events.

The procedure was designed by Jeffrey Mitchell (1983) and specifies that all members of a group, who have been affected by a specific traumatic event, should attend and follow a standard seven-phase discussion that lasts between one and three hours. Many service organizations have adopted this model or other similar debriefing procedures, as their standard way of helping staff deal with highly stressful events.

While many people have found these debriefing procedures very helpful for their speedy adjustment and return to work, there has recently been some debate, and several reviews published (e.g. Rose and Bisson, 1998), as to whether debriefing can actually help prevent the later development of longer-term psychological problems, including Post-Traumatic Stress Disorder (PTSD). Some people argue that, in certain cases, especially if used too early, the procedures may even result in more damaging, rather than helpful, effects. Whilst there is unified agreement that help needs to be made available for people who have to deal with highly stressful events as part of their work, there are now more indications that the type of help needs to be tailored, not just to each individual event but to the needs of each particular location and to each individual within it as well. In future, effective trauma after-care for workers in this field will need to become even more sophisticated and may need, once more, to draw on the expertise of qualified and highly trained professionals, rather than on people who have been limited in their training to apply one standard intervention procedure only.

If you belong to one of these trauma care response groups and you have experienced any signs of vicarious traumatization or other reactions, you may find it helpful to read and work through the rest of this book. If your reactions persist, you would also be advised to seek out a trauma specialist, who can offer you individually tailored professional help.

PART TWO

Managing Traumatic Stress

5

Moving Towards Your Path of Recovery

A Framework for Healing

If you have been distressed for a long time, or if your reactions following a recent traumatic experience have been particularly intense, or again, if your symptoms did improve but then recently returned with a disturbing intensity, you may have turned directly to this section of the book and not bothered to read the chapters in the first part.

The temptation to seek the practical strategies first is very understandable; your world has probably felt so out of control that you want to fix it as quickly as possible. Nevertheless, you need a framework from which to apply these practical strategies for symptom management. At the very least you should have read Chapter 2, 'Understanding Your Symptoms', so that you are aware of the 'why' as well as the 'how to' in symptom management.

This book is not designed to offer a 'quick fix' (although some of our techniques may make a considerable difference for you right away, the first or second time you try them). Rather, we hope to provide a lasting improvement, and that can only be achieved by acting on the (cognitive-behavioral) techniques which this book proposes.

Working actively will mean writing things down, not just keeping them in your head. This will help to stop the same thoughts circling inside your head in repetitive, negative patterns. An alternative to writing might be to tape-record your thoughts and reactions. Sometimes drawing pictures or diagrams, or creating a collage or producing a clay model (if you like doing art), or even creating music (if you can play an instrument) can be therapeutic ways of expressing what you have been feeling. Reorganizing your life or even just changing the location of furniture in a room may help you to see things a bit differently.

Preparing Your Path to Recovery

Rather than just starting immediately with the practical exercises it is usually helpful to take a little time to prepare yourself for the changes you are about to make.

For most people change takes place in gradual stages that build on each other. As progress is made, it is quite common to forget where you started and therefore how far you have already advanced and changed on the way.

Look back to the example of Harry in Chapter 1. Harry described his process of recovery like climbing out of a deep, waterless well. While he was climbing up the well, he sometimes thought it would be safer for him to go back right to the bottom where he started. This seemed an easier option at times than continuing his climb upwards. This was partly because he could not recognize at the time how far he had already managed to climb. All he could see was the potential danger that might lie ahead, but not the danger he had already successfully mastered and left behind in the bottom. To avoid falling into the same trap as Harry, decide to keep a record that reminds you of the progress you are making over time.

> Get yourself a special notebook that you only use for making notes about your personal recovery process. It's a good idea, too, to date all your entries in the notebook.

Devise a Schedule of Positive Self-care

Recovery does not happen by magic; it involves hard work, for example, facing unpleasant memories instead of avoiding them.

To be successful and to accelerate your own healing so that you can feel more in control of your life, it is very important to commit yourself to a schedule of positive self-care throughout the recovery process. This should include:

• Allowing yourself time for your recovery work
• Setting aside time for relaxation and nurturing
• Keeping a notebook throughout your journey of recovery
• Sticking to the contract that you make with yourself
• Taking personal responsibility for ensuring your own safety
• Controlling destructive impulses, not indulging suicidal thoughts (or seeking immediate professional help if they persist)
• Removing anything dangerous or potentially harmful from your home
• Not abusing alcohol or any drugs.

Identify which obstacles you need to remove or which things in your life you must change so that you will be ready to commit to this schedule of positive self-care.

Make a Contract With Yourself

The first thing that you should set down in your new notebook is a contract with yourself. This will help you start off with the best recovery conditions for yourself.

Read and work through these steps to assist in making this contract with yourself:

1 Take some time to think about what your life is like at the moment. Think about all those things that might make it difficult for you to commit yourself to your own process of recovery. List them under 'Obstacles to Recovery' in your notebook:

   a. First, think about all the *external* obstacles that might stand in your way of recovery. These might include: too little time in the day; too many conflicting pressures due to other commitments, like work or children; other people or partners are not supportive; physically you can't get about very well at the moment; you use alcohol or drugs to help you cope with your pain, etc. Write these down.

b. Second, think about all the *internal* obstacles that might be hindering you in your process of recovery. These might be: being too fearful of change; lacking in motivation and energy; being too critical and undermining yourself; never giving yourself praise for any of your achievements, etc. Write these down.

2 Now look at all the obstacles that you have identified and ask yourself how you could reorganize or change aspects of your life to reduce some of these obstacles. For example, if you have too little time in your day, you might need to think about your real priorities at the moment. You may find that your own process of recovery is rather more important than some of those other things that have occupied so much time and become part of your routine. If this is the case, work on restructuring your time and reorganizing your activities.

a. If other people or your partner are not supportive, think of ways in which they might become *more* supportive of you. For example, do they really understand what you are going through at the moment? Would it help to show them this book to see if that changes their approach? Even if you find that they remain unsupportive, you can still think about ways in which you could succeed without their help.

b. If you know that you are too critical and undermining of yourself, make a commitment to monitor the times when you tell yourself off or think badly about yourself. Keep a record and write down the critical or negative things that you say to yourself. Ask yourself if saying these things makes it more likely that you will succeed with your tasks or less likely? Then try and say something to yourself that gives you a better chance of success. For example, you might say, 'I can only try and do my best under the circumstances'.

You may not be able to lift every obstacle that stands in your way, but try to remove as many as you can at the outset of your recovery process. Write down *what* changes you want to make to remove as many obstacles as possible, and how and when you intend to make these changes.

3 Now make a list of promises to yourself that will aid in your process of recovery. These may well be things that you are not doing at the moment.

Your list might look like this:

a. I promise to commit myself to my own process of recovery. I will try to make those changes that feel helpful to me and set aside time to do so.

b. I promise to be honest with myself, even if this means facing things that require more effort from me or feelings that are a little uncomfortable.

c. I will give myself a chance and persevere in my efforts. I understand that the process of recovery will take time and I will allow myself as much time as I need for this. I will not expect techniques to work the first time I use them, but I will stick with them and try them out over a longer period of time. I will tailor them to fit my own needs and situation.

d. I will listen to myself and recognize my limits. I will not push myself unduly and will pace myself in my efforts. I know that it is better to work at things in a steady and planned way rather than trying to solve everything at once.

e. I will give myself regular breaks and time off for relaxation or nurturing activities. I will aim to achieve a healthy balance in my life, where I take regular breaks and pursue activities that are nurturing and relaxing for myself. These will help me in my process of recovery.

f. I promise to do those things that are helpful to me and not those that could put me or other people in danger. This includes a promise to myself that I will not use alcohol or drugs to block out my feelings of pain or discomfort.

g. I have read the Cautions at the end of Chapter 1 (page 14) of this book and I will stop if any of the exercises cause me unbearable distress. I will seek professional help if I can't progress on my own or if I am a danger to others or myself.

(Your signature, dated)

The preceding list is not exhaustive and you may want to include other promises that will help you in your recovery. Taking responsibility in this way is the first positive step on the path to recovery!

6

On the Path to Recovery

Processing Your Experience – Telling the Story!

If you have followed the above preparations you are now ready
to take your first step towards healing and to unlock some of
those aspects of your trauma that you may have kept secret from
yourself or others, or that you have simply avoided confronting.
This chapter should help you with this process in a practical
way. The exercises should only be undertaken if you have made
the necessary preparations suggested in Chapter 5 and if your
trauma is no longer present as a daily reality in your life.

Keeping Secrets

Most people have to face a barrage of questions during the time
immediately after their trauma. These questions can come from
relatives and friends as well as from emergency and rescue workers, such as police, firemen, ambulance personnel, nurses or
doctors at the hospital, your own medical practitioner and even
sometimes the press. At the same time, most people feel very
shocked and stunned in this initial period after their trauma
and find it difficult to cope with questions.

Such questions may be experienced as very intrusive and
inappropriate, and it is only natural for trauma sufferers to want
to keep their responses brief.

There might also have been some other reasons that prevented
you from sharing your true feelings with others:

• A feeling that although people asked you questions, they didn't really want to know the full details, perhaps because they felt uncomfortable being confronted by the horror of your experiences.

- Some people said very tactless and completely inappropriate things, which upset you. You didn't feel strong enough to let them know that the things they were saying hurt you or may even have made the trauma worse, and instead you just closed down and refused to share things with them at all.

- Some only talked about the physical aspects, about your injuries or wounds, but completely discounted how the trauma affected you emotionally.

- Other people may have asked you about your feelings, but you felt uncomfortable opening up to them. You may have felt you should be brave or that it was a sign of weakness if you allowed yourself to share with them what you really felt. Another possibility is that you felt you shouldn't upset or burden them with some of the distressing experiences you had.

- It could also be that people really cared and asked you lots of helpful questions about your feelings, but that at the time you just felt completely numb, and couldn't respond. You may have still been too shocked to feel anything or to verbalize your feelings.

- People were too preoccupied caring for others, who were also involved in the trauma, or suffered as a result of it, and completely ignored you because they thought you were all right. Maybe your injuries weren't as serious as other people's; maybe others died and you didn't.

- Either you or other people felt you were to blame or were responsible for the trauma because of some action you took. As a result nobody showed any sympathy for the physical or emotional effects on you.

The following example illustrates one aspect of why people are reluctant to share their true feelings:

> 'Pete had been in a fire caused by a gas explosion at his work in a biscuit factory. He was one of the few survivors to sustain only minor physical injuries and, immediately following the explosion, he was responsible for rescuing others, who were

trapped by collapsed parts of the building and needed pulling out before the fire could reach them. When emergency personnel arrived they took over from him, concentrating all their efforts on those that seemed worse off. Pete, although very badly shocked and exhausted from his rescue attempts, was put in a safe corner of a nearby building that served as a rescue shelter and given little attention. After a physical examination and some minor wound care at his local hospital he was discharged. Members of his family were very pleased that he hadn't been hurt more seriously and they kept saying to him how lucky he was to have got away with it so lightly. His family seemed more concerned about his other colleagues, some of whom were also personal friends, who were still in hospital with severe physical injuries. Even the fire investigation officer, the police, his boss and the owner of the factory, who later came to talk to him to take a statement of his account of events, thanked him for his rescue attempts but disregarded his feelings during or after the trauma. They repeatedly emphasized how lucky he could count himself not to have been one of the people whom the trauma had hit more seriously. Pete secretly felt guilty about 'having got away with it so lightly' and ashamed about the continuous upsetting thoughts and feelings about the trauma that kept intruding into his mind day and night completely out of the blue. Even four weeks later he hadn't had a single night's peaceful sleep, was suffering from terrible nightmares and felt emotionally extremely distressed. He felt very bad about these feelings as he thought he should be grateful that he was one of the lucky ones. Secretly he thought that he was going mad and he hated himself for his weakness. He kept completely silent about his feelings because he felt he had no right to seek anybody else's support, when most of his colleagues were so much worse off.'

Pete

Opening Up

In order to work through, come to terms with and resolve a trauma, it is really important that all aspects of it are processed. This means that you need to make sense of:

- what exactly happened
- how you reacted
- what it meant to you.

The above example illustrates how people can be affected by a trauma in very different ways. There is no prescribed way of reacting to a trauma and, while for some people their physical injuries are the most painful, for others their emotional wounds are far greater. Your experience of the trauma is unique to you and a recognition of this helps you to re-establish control and positively change the deeply unsettling and disruptive effect the trauma may have had on you.

There are many ways in which you can make sense of your trauma and often it can be enough to talk about it in detail to a person or friend whom you can trust. When you do this it is normal that you should experience quite strong emotions and even some of the physical reactions that you felt during the time of the trauma. If this happens, allow these feelings their space – they are an important part of the normal healing process. To keep feelings from becoming too overwhelming, ensure that you keep yourself safe while going through your experiences.

How to Process and Make Sense of Your Experience

Even if you do not feel able to share your experiences with others, you need to find other ways of processing your experience. Some alternatives are suggested below.

1 *Write an account of your own personal trauma*
You could think of this account like a personal 'testimony' to the world, so that others could witness it and understand the terrible experience you have gone through. It might help to think of it as being similar to the way in which the people in this book have shared their experiences in order to help you understand and recover from your trauma better.

How to prepare your account:

a. *Only work on your trauma if it is actually over*, so, for example, a road traffic accident that took place three weeks ago or a bank robbery four months ago. If your trauma is still with you, for example, if a person who has hurt you is still around and continues to hurt you or could hurt you, then do not attempt to work through your experience at the moment, as it will not be beneficial.

b. *Set aside a limited amount of time each day, at a specific time, and arrange to do a pleasurable activity afterwards.* This should be a time when you are not disrupted by others and when you can feel safe expressing some of the emotions that come up. Set yourself a time limit of about 45 minutes to one hour. If you haven't finished writing your account at the end of the time for that day, jot down a few notes and resume the next day. It is important that you stop after the time limit that you have set for yourself. Afterwards you should have arranged to do a personally pleasurable activity, such as meeting with a friend, taking the dog for a walk, listening to some music, going to church, taking a relaxing bath, arranging for an aromatherapy massage – or whatever else that is likely to be helpful to you.

c. *Allow yourself as much time for recounting the whole of your trauma as you need.* You may need several days or possibly several weeks until you have completely accounted for all aspects of your experience. It is important that you don't rush things and that you always stop after the time limit you have set yourself for the day. Don't be impatient with yourself – there is no standard guideline about how long it should take you to work through your trauma. It is a good idea, though, to work on this for a set period of time each day. If you need longer than a week you might like to give yourself a day off from it at the weekend, before starting on it again the following week. If you have to miss a day because of other commitments, just carry on the following day.

d. *Include as much information and detail about the trauma as possible.* It is important that you think about everything that you saw, smelled, heard, touched and sensed around you at the time. Remember that this experience was unique to you, no other person would have experienced the trauma in exactly the way in which you did. Even if at first you think that you don't recall very much, when you allow yourself to revisit the experience, it is often surprising how many things your mind and body *have* registered, often over a very short period of time.

e. *Write in the present tense, using the first person.* Start your account at a time shortly before the trauma happened and continue to work through all aspects, including the aftermath, such as rescue attempts, your experiences at hospital, how others reacted, etc. Write your account in the *first person* as if you were really revisiting your trauma, for example: 'As I see ... I go to ... and I feel ... ' This will help to make your account more vivid. In your account work through:

- What exactly happened, i.e. start with the facts: what were you doing and thinking just before the event? Go through the entire sequence of events until the aftermath.
- How you reacted, i.e. what were your feelings? What did you do? What physical sensations did you notice?
- What it meant to you, what was the worst part for you? How have you changed? What is your life like now?, What can't or won't you do now that you used to do before? What things or people aren't there anymore because of the trauma? What is the hardest part for you to get used to? Where are you stuck at the moment? What needs to happen for this stuckness to be resolved?

f. *Allow yourself to experience the feelings and sensations that may arise.* Traumatic experiences wouldn't affect us if we didn't have feelings. It is very important that you acknowledge the presence of these feelings and bodily sensations, for example, feeling hot or cold, etc. To do so is an essential part of the processing of the experience.

It is important not to be frightened, even if these feelings surprise you by their strength. Remind yourself that this is how you felt at the time of the trauma but that is past. These reactions are simply part of your own coping responses and are designed to help you survive the trauma as best you can.

It is quite normal that you should have had very strong and often confusing reactions both during and after your trauma. It is also entirely normal that you may have felt, said or done things during the trauma that you would never have done under ordinary circumstances. Some people feel that the trauma has brought out characteristics in them that they didn't know they had. If you feel ashamed, angry or guilty about having reacted in a particular way during the trauma, remember that you reacted in the only way you could at the time. With hindsight what you did may not seem right to you, you feel you should have acted differently or done more. This is a very common reaction. It is important to remind yourself that during the trauma you reacted under the conditions of a life-threatening experience and that at the time and under those conditions, for you, those were the only things that you *could* do. This doesn't necessarily make those decisions that you took morally or legally right, but it puts them into a realistic perspective.

Caution: Stop writing if any of your feelings become too overwhelming. Take a break and distract yourself with something unconnected to the trauma. If your reactions continue to cause you distress, make sure that you seek professional help.

---

2   *Other ways of processing your experience*

There are other ways of processing your experiences if you find writing difficult. Follow the same guidelines as above (a–f) and choose one of the alternative methods, outlined below:

- Use a tape recorder to dictate your experiences on tape. Then listen to it being played back to you.
- Paint or draw. You don't have to be very artistic, but sometimes it can help to express all your experiences in the form of a drawing or painting. It doesn't have to be an accurate representation of what went on, but it should capture the

personal meaning for you and reflect all the feelings and sensations that you experienced. Allow yourself to express all the imagery that comes up for you when you revisit your trauma.

- Make a collage. Use anything you can find, such as old magazines, old clothing material, wood, threads, colors, etc. to build up a representation of what happened to you. Again, the aim is not to create a fantastic piece of art, but rather to capture the meaning of the trauma for you in the collage.
- Write a poem or a song. If you have a bit of literary talent or if you are musical you might find it healing to express and process your experience in this way. Try to come up with a series of verses in your poem or your song as you process your experience over several days.
- Make a sculpture, using modeling clay or other bits of material.

The important thing is to allow yourself to be as creative as you can. The aim is to process exactly what has happened to you, how you reacted and what it meant to you. Choose whichever method feels most helpful to you. You can even use more than one method. You may have hobbies that you haven't used for a while, such as wood carving or working with stained glass, that can help you represent your feelings now.

Follow the principles outlined above and make sure you have a clear beginning and an end to this process. Later, when you feel you have advanced in your healing process and nearly recovered, you may want to mark your journey in a similarly creative way by trying some of the suggestions made in Chapter 14.

When you have completed this first step toward recovery and healing, reward yourself for your achievement!

7

Managing Your Intrusive, Re-experiencing Reactions

What Seems Right is Not Necessarily the Most Helpful!

As most of us know from everyday life, when something is on our minds so much that we can't stop thinking about it, feel taken over by it or find ourselves ruminating about it at inappropriate moments, it is usually ineffective just to tell ourselves to forget about it. Trying to suppress a worry or an obsessive idea often causes it to rebound even more strongly.

Most of us have had the experience of being dumped by a boy- or a girlfriend at some stage in our lives. Do you remember the very first time this happened to you? It would probably have been in one of your early relationships. Do you still remember why the person dumped you at the time? Can you recall how you coped with this then? Like most people, you may have wanted to put this experience behind you as quickly as possible in order to get on with other things in your life. You may have gone to school or work as usual, trying to push it out of your mind and not to think about it any more. If you used that strategy, can you remember if it actually worked for you at the time? Could you successfully push the feelings and thoughts about that experience out of your mind – or did you find that trying not to think about it made it harder for you and thoughts kept intruding anyway, distracting you from what you wanted to get on with?

Most people find that trying not to think about something makes them think even more about it – it makes the thought stronger. It is the same with traumatic thoughts and memories.

A scientist called Wegner (1989) found that thoughts that have been deliberately pushed away occur about twice as often as thoughts that haven't been suppressed. Nevertheless, this is precisely what many people try to do after a trauma. A very common strategy used by those suffering from post-trauma reactions is to 'try not to think about it', 'try to put it out of my mind', 'try to avoid reminders of it that would make me think about it'. Horowitz's Impact of Events Scale (1979) is a questionnaire that is used to measure post-traumatic stress reactions. It asks how people cope with thoughts about their trauma and looks at how often people tend to use the 'not thinking about it strategy'. It uses this as a way of measuring the severity of a person's distress. The more often these strategies need to be used, the more severe the intrusive reactions are likely to be.

Getting to Know Your Intrusive (Re-experiencing) Reactions

In order to be able to manage these intrusive and re-experiencing reactions, you need to be aware how frequent and how upsetting to you they are. Measuring the frequency and the level of upset will enable you to take what is called a *baseline*. This is the measure of your reactions *before* you start to make any changes and has several advantages.

1 When you have made changes you then take another measure to establish whether the changes you have made have helped to lessen your reactions.
2 As you advance in your healing you will see that the gap between your baseline score and subsequent scores will get wider. This is a recognition of the improvements that you have made.
3 You will also become aware if certain strategies are not helping – by an increase in your score compared to your score at the baseline. *If that is the case you must stop the strategies that you have been using and seek professional help.*

Copy these questions into your notebook, date the entry and try to answer them as best as you can. The scales 0–3 are explained below:

- To rate how frequently you have had each of the experiences over the past week, use the following 0–3 scale:

0	1	2	3
Not at all	Once a week/ A little bit/ Once in a while	2–4 times per week/ Somewhat/ Half the time	5 times per week/ Very much/ Almost always

- To rate how upsetting each of the experiences has been in the past week, use the following 0–3 scale:

0	1	2	3
Not at all upsetting	Quite upsetting	Very upsetting	Extremely upsetting

Please answer the following questions by circling the number on each scale that best applies to you:

1 In the past 7 days have thoughts or images (including smells or sounds) about your traumatic experience intruded into your mind at times when you did not want them to?

How frequently? 0 1 2 3   How upsetting has this been? 0 1 2 3

2 In the past 7 days have you experienced disturbing dreams or nightmares about your traumatic experience?

How frequently? 0 1 2 3   How upsetting has this been? 0 1 2 3

3 In the past 7 days have you had flashbacks or the feeling that you are acting a part or the sense that the trauma is happening all over again?

How frequently? 0 1 2 3   How upsetting has this been? 0 1 2 3

4 In the past 7 days have you become very unsettled emotionally when reminded of your traumatic experience (very sad, tearful, angry, fearful, anxious, etc.)?

How frequently? 0 1 2 3   How upsetting has this been? 0 1 2 3

5 In the past 7 days have you noticed uncomfortable physical reactions (for example, headaches, breaking out in sweat, heart beating fast, unable to catch your breath, clumsiness) when you were reminded of your traumatic experience?

How frequently? o 1 2 3   How upsetting has this been? o 1 2 3

Once you have circled the number that best applies to you on each question, both on the frequency and the upset ratings, add the scores from all the questions (1–5) for each of the two categories. Record these total scores in your notebook.

INTRUSIVE, RE-EXPERIENCING REACTIONS ON .... (date)

Your total score for
frequency is: ....   If your total scores
                                             on both measures are:
                                             5 or below = they are low
Your total score for   5 – 10 = they fall into
upset is: ....   the mid-range
                                             10 or more = they are high

---

Lastly, give an overall rating for how disabling these intrusive, re-experiencing reactions have been to you in the past week by circling the number that applies to you on the scale used below (you could also copy this into your notebook):

o	1	2	3	4	5	6	7	8

Not at all disabling	Slightly disabling	Definitely disabling	Markedly disabling	Severely disabling

Now that you have established your baseline for intrusive (re-experiencing) reactions, you can begin to try to reduce both the frequency and the upset rates of your responses. If you have scored in the high range, you might find that professional help would really be useful to you, in addition to working through this book.

The Difference between a Flashback and an Intrusive Memory

Intrusive memories are vivid pictures, smells, sounds, etc. that are experienced as being very real, although the individual remains aware that they are actually recollections (often very disturbing ones) of what happened before and during the traumatic event. Intrusive memories can often produce intense physical sensations and it is very common for people to try and block these memories out or push them away when they occur.

During a flashback, the trauma, or some aspect of the traumatic event, is experienced *as if it were happening all over again*. You might re-experience sights, sounds, the presence of others, smells, things touching or hitting you. Any sensory information registered in your memory may be replayed vividly. Reactions like these tend to make people feel like they are 'losing their minds', or that their minds are playing tricks on them: they know logically the event can't be happening again, yet it seems to be. Flashbacks can be truly terrifying, because of their unpredictability and the accompanying feeling of being out of control.

Both intrusive memories and flashbacks can be triggered by very subtle reminders in the everyday environment, such as a brief sound, a smell, or just a feeling. The experience both of intrusive memories and flashbacks can make you feel very much out of control, especially because they seem to come totally out of the blue and can elicit such strong physical reactions. Now we will look at strategies for managing these intrusive memories and flashbacks. The aim will be to help you learn how to gain more and more control over them. The first step, as always, is for you to find out and understand what is happening. Second, we will introduce you to techniques to help you master some of these distressing intrusive reactions. Although examining and confronting intrusive reactions can make you feel uncomfortable, it is usually not harmful or dangerous so please allow yourself to be as open as possible as you begin these exercises.

First, a couple of ground rules:

• Work at your own pace and don't push yourself too hard. This is not a race!

- *Caution*: Stop the exercises and distract yourself if you are unable to tolerate the strength of the physical sensations that are called up. Try the exercise again another day and focus on reducing these physical sensations to a tolerable level. If your reactions persist or get worse, seek professional help.

Managing Intrusive Memories

As we have seen, trying to block out your intrusive memories is not necessarily the most helpful approach. It would be more constructive for you to learn strategies to enable you to integrate them into your life in a gradual way. Work through the following exercise to help you to ascertain just how often you try to dismiss your traumatic memories.

Exercise 1

1 Do this exercise when you have an hour to concentrate on yourself.
2 Take your notebook and draw a table, similar to the one in the Example Record below (blank copies are provided in the Appendix).
3 Look at your watch and note down the time.
4 Then get on with your activities as you normally would. For the next hour observe whenever a thought or feeling about your traumatic experience pops into your mind. Each time it does, notice how you react. Try and rate the strength of your distress on a scale 0–8 (see below).
5 Also note how you are trying to cope with the memory. If you find yourself automatically trying to push it from your mind, make a tick in that column of your table. Stop yourself after an hour.
6 At the end of this hour check to see how often you tried *not* to think about it, when an intrusive memory about the trauma popped into your mind.

continued on next page

Rate your strength of distress on the following scale:

```
  0     1     2     3     4     5     6     7     8
●───────────────────────────────────────────────●
  No          A little      Definite      Marked        Severe
distress      distress      distress      distress      distress
```

Here is an Example Record:

Date: _21.12.1998_   Time: _11.15am._

Time	Intrusive Memory	Sensations in your body	Strength of Distress (0–10)	Able to tolerate it	Push it away
11.20	Thought about the ice on the road before the car slipped	Tightening of Chest, faster Breathing	4 Definite distress	✓	
11.35	Smell of burnt rubber (know it's from the accident)	Sense of Headache, nausea	7 Severe distress		✓
11.40	Image of other car	Feeling sick	6 Marked distress	✓	

What did you observe from your own record? Was the result as you had expected? Or were you surprised at how often you push memories away? Note down your findings in your notebook, being aware also of bodily sensations and the level of distress the intrusions caused. At what level of distress did you find it hard to tolerate the intrusions?

You will probably have noticed from the exercise that different memories can cause different levels of distress. Not all of them are equally strong in terms of how they affect you.

You are probably also aware that the less distressing a memory the better you are able to tolerate it and the less you want to suppress it. The next exercise offers some strategies for integrating intrusive memories rather than suppressing them.

Exercise 2

This exercise helps you learn, at a gradual pace, how to accept more and more of the intrusive memories into your life. You need to allow about half an hour a day on a regular basis for this exercise.

From your observations in the last exercise note *at what rate of distress you feel unable to tolerate your intrusive memories and start pushing them away.* In the example in Exercise 1, the person could still tolerate her intrusive memories at a strength rating of 4. However, 6 was too high for her to tolerate the distress and at that level she pushed the memories away. Her physical sensation at that level was feeling sick.

1 Write down in your notebook what physical sensations you notice at the level where you start to push your memories away.

2 Now focus on your body and see whether you can make your body feel those sensations. Although this might be a little uncomfortable, it is not dangerous! Just allow yourself to stay with those sensations as long as you can. Just notice them and feel them. Try to stay as calm and relaxed as you can. Say to yourself that this is how your body feels when it experiences that strength of distress.

3 Some people also find it helpful to think of these bodily feelings as a shape or a specific color. Try to do that: if you can think of them as a colored shape, explore making that shape bigger or smaller and see whether you can change its form or color at the same time. Write this down in your notebook as you go along.

4 The longer you can allow yourself to feel your physical sensations, the more you will realize that tolerating them *is* possible for you, even if it feels a little uncomfortable.

5 Perform this exercise for several days, for half an hour at a time.

continued on next page

6 After you have learned to tolerate your bodily sensations at that level of strength, repeat Exercise 1 to measure your distress levels.

7 After a while, if you notice that you no longer need to push away the intrusive memories that cause you this level of distress, try Exercise 2 again, moving onto the next higher level of strength of distress.

8 If you find that you still need to push those intrusive memories away, go back to Exercise 2 and stay with it for a bit longer until you can move onto 6.

Managing Flashbacks

One of the most distressing aspects of a flashback is its unpredictability and its potentially overwhelming strength. Your flashbacks may feel to you as uncontrollable as a nightmare and indeed, flashbacks have been described as 'waking nightmares' (Meichenbaum, 1994).

Rather than letting them control you, you need to find ways of controlling your flashbacks, as you did with the intrusive memories.

Step 1: Getting to Know Your Flashbacks and Listening to Your Body's Responses

Exercise 3

The first step is for you to notice and understand what happens to you while you experience a flashback. Think back to the last time you had a flashback or alternatively, wait until you experience the next one. Copy the questions from the boxes below into your notebook and answer them (additional copies are provided in the Appendix).

continued on next page

A. Recognize the triggers:	Record your observations:
1 When did it happen?	
2 What were you doing at the time?	
3 What else was going on when it started?	
4 Was anybody else with you?	
5 Can you recognize any similarities between your current situation and the situation that you were transported to in your flashback?	
6 Can you remember when you have felt this way before?	
7 What is similar and what is different to the previous situation/s?	
8 What do you think trig-gered it? (For example, thoughts, smells, sounds, pictures, feelings, taste – or reminders such as conversations, media or special events, such as anniversaries.)	

B. Identify the traumatic memory:	Record your observations:
1 What do you remember about your flashback?	
2 Even if it feels a little distressing, describe in as much detail as you can what went through your mind.	
3 Can you describe or draw the images that you saw during your flashback?	
4 Do you know how long it lasted?	
5 Were you noticing what was going on around you or did the flashback block everything else out?	

Rate your strength of feelings on the following scale:

```
0    1    2    3    4    5    6    7    8
●─────────────────────────────────────●
No        A little    Definite    Marked      Severe
distress  distress    distress    distress    distress
```

C. Get to know your body's responses:	Record your observations:
1 What sensations did you notice in your body during the flashback?	
2 Try and describe them in as much detail as you can.	
3 How strong were these sensations? Can you try and give them a rating between 0 to 8 (using the above scale)?	
4 What were your thoughts about these sensations?	
5 How did you react and respond to those sensations in your body?	
6 What actions did you take to make yourself feel better?	
7 Can you think of other ways you may have used to control flashbacks in the past?	

Having answered these questions in your notebook, start a diary to monitor your flashbacks. The more thoroughly you understand them, the more likely it is you will learn to control them.

Understanding Flashbacks

Every flashback has three stages (Meichenbaum, 1994). The first is the trigger stage. This tells you what started it in the first place. Triggers are different for each person and therefore it is important that you try and work out what the special triggers might be for you. (This could also be useful for controlling your intrusive memories.) Triggers can be thoughts, images, sounds, smells, something someone does or says, tastes, special events, currently stressful situations, financial or medical problems, and many more. Make a list of what you believe to be your most common triggers, in Exercise 4 below.

Exercise 4

I have identified the following, most common triggers for my flashbacks:

_____

_____

_____

_____

_____

_____

_____

_____

_____

_____

_____

The second stage consists of the 'surfacing of memories' during the flashback. These are the upsetting memories that make you feel as if you are reliving aspects of the trauma. They can seem so real and their images can be so sharp and acute, that you may feel that you are right back in the actual trauma. You may literally feel as if you are 'taken over' by these memories and that you stop all other activities while you are experiencing the flashback. Traumatic memories take the form of visual images but can be accompanied by sounds, smells, tastes and other physical sensations. The flashbacks usually last between a few seconds and a few minutes, but when they are really severe they can last more than one hour.

The third stage is the 'aftermath' of the flashback. At this stage the person will often still feel very strong physical sensations. Some people find that their breathing increases, others notice that they are feeling cold and shivery or very hot or that their heartbeat is rapid. Often people can have very strong emotional responses to the flashback itself, getting very angry, for example, or feeling very sad and distressed. The feelings can be disorientating: if you have stopped all other activities during the flashback it can then be hard to remember what was said or went on during the current episode of your flashback. This is more likely to happen if a flashback lasts longer than a few minutes.

It is important to remember that flashbacks are your mind's way of trying to make sense of what has happened to you. They are a common reaction and therefore you do not need to feel frightened by them. Like other PTSD symptoms, they are an indication of 'unfinished' business, suggesting that further healing needs to occur before the impact of the trauma can be resolved. Exercise 5 demonstrates what you can do to increase understanding of your flashbacks:

Exercise 5

Below is an example of a simple flashback record chart. Copy the chart into your notebook and then use it to monitor your own flashbacks over a longer period of time. The longer you monitor your flashbacks the better the understanding you are likely to gain of them. You might also like to refer to the questions you asked yourself in Exercise 3 when you are using this chart (blank copies are provided in the Appendix).

Flashback Recording Chart

Rate your Strength of Responses on the following scale:

0	1	2	3	4	5	6	7	8
No distress		A little distress		Definite distress		Marked distress		Severe distress

Date/ Time	Trigger (external and internal)	Traumatic memory (content)	Your reactions (physical & emotional responses), Rate their strength (0–8)	Duration of flashback
12.3.98 6.30p.m.	Electricity goes off — Lights go off due to a short power-cut in this area	Takes me back to the time when the lights went off during my solitary confinement after being taken a prisoner	Fear. Feeling of being out of control. Feeling of coldness. Shivering all over my body. Severe distress = 7	20 min. — lost touch with surroundings
14.3.98 11.15a.m.	Backdoor was open — Tom walks in Without ringing bell	People would just come in and I never had any control over it	Shouted at Tom. Increased heartbeat Definite distress = 4	1 min. —
14.3.98 1.00p.m.	Maggie cooked lunch. — Smell of onions in the house.	Can see person who interrogated me. His breath smelt of onions.	Feeling of nausea and sickness, had to walk out of house. Marked distress = 6	5 min. — took time to shake off face
15.3.98 2.30p.m.	Went to visit mum. Toby (dog) moved out from under the sofa one of his favorite places)	Set off a flashback to the time in combat when someone shot at me from under a car	Terrified, nearly killed Toby. Had a real go at mum. Took me ages to calm down Severe distress = 8	3 min. — took long time to calm down after
17.3.98 9.00p.m.	Invited to party. Fireworks display.	The sound brought me right back to my experiences under combat fire.	Terrified, nearly wetted myself, heart pounding, lost it with friends — shouted Severe distress = 8	10 min. — friends had to stop fireworks

Step 2: Finding the most helpful ways to deal with your flashbacks

The more you are able to monitor when your flashbacks happen, and what they are like, the more familiar you will become with them. Once you can recognize a flashback and notice your reaction you are ready to try to gain more control over them. This is not an easy process and most people find that it takes time to learn to do so. It is important that you give yourself a chance and persevere even if things don't work immediately. Here are some exercises that should help you control your flashbacks.

Exercise 6: Avoiding the triggers

One way of controlling flashbacks is to avoid certain situations or thoughts that are known triggers for your flashbacks. This can be very helpful, especially if some triggers cause such strong responses in you that you, or others around you, do not always feel safe when they occur.

Go back over your notes from Exercise 4 and Exercise 5 and highlight those triggers it would be helpful for you to avoid.

Make a new list in your notebook like the one below and plan what you might do to avoid those triggers you have identified:

Example record:

List of Triggers to avoid:	My plan of what I can do to avoid them:
Firework displays	*I will avoid public firework display when I know about them*
	I will check with friends beforehand if there is going to be a firework display at their party. I will explain my problems to them and ask them to excuse me if I have to leave a little earlier, before the display starts.

Remember: The use of avoidance strategies can be helpful under certain circumstances because you have to protect yourself from the strong reactions that a flashback can trigger (including behavior that could be unpleasant or dangerous to others). However, it is probably not helpful to use only avoidance strategies, especially if, in order to avoid a potential trigger, you have to forego situations that under other circumstances would be pleasurable for you.

Exercise 7: Categorizing your triggers

Look again at your notes from Exercises 4 and 5. Now try and divide as many of the triggers that you have identified into the four groups outlined below.

Example record:

Least difficult   most difficult

1 Triggers that I might be able to handle now	2 Triggers that I can't cope with yet, but I may be able to handle soon (maybe in a few weeks' or months' time)	3 Triggers that seem really hard to gain control over at the moment, but that I would eventually like to tackle	4 Triggers that I will always want to avoid (for my own and others' safety)
e.g.: leaving backdoor open when I am around and allowing family to walk in without shouting at them	*e.g.: smell of onions during cooking*	*e.g.: things jumping out from underneath objects (e.g. mum's dog or in other situations)*	*e.g.: Firework displays*

Now that you have classed your triggers into easy and hard ones, choose one target trigger that you think you might be able to handle now and try out some of the strategies in Exercises 8 and 9 below.

Exercise 8: Working with a target trigger

Different management strategies

1 Rescript your memory
   a. Write down in as much detail as possible the flashback memory that normally occurs in response to this trigger.
   b. Ask yourself what the most distressing aspect of this flashback memory is. Write down why this affects you so much.
   c. Describe the sensations that this flashback memory sets off in you.
   d. Now think of a way in which you could rescript the flashback to make it less distressing to you. Is there is anything in this imagery that you could change so that you would feel more in control?
   e. Rewrite the flashback memory including this changed image.
   f. Imagine yourself experiencing the flashback in this changed form.
   g. Then rescript this flashback each time it is set off by your identified target trigger.

2 Resize your memory and watch it like a film
   a. Follow steps a to c as above.
   b. Now try and imagine watching your flashback memory like a film. See if you can reduce its image in size so that it would fit onto a small television screen.
   c. Practise watching this as often as possible. Slow down the speed of the film, or 'freeze' frames if you wish. 'Grey' down the color.
   d. Then practise watching your flashback in this way, when your identified trigger sets it off.

Once you have mastered more control over this identified target trigger and feel fairly comfortable about tolerating it, you can then select a different target trigger to work on.

Exercise 9 offers some techniques for you to try out when you feel very disconnected during a flashback. They will help to connect you more to the present and therefore make you feel more in control.

Exercise 9: Some grounding techniques

Grounding techniques can help bring you back into the present if you have become disconnected from reality during a flashback. They shift your focus away from the flashback and reduce its intensity.

1 As soon as you notice the first signs of a flashback, focus on any object in your environment around you. Look at the chosen object and describe to yourself:
   - its color
   - its shape and size
   - its texture (go over to it if you can and feel it)
   - its age and what it might be used for
   - what you like or dislike about it.

2 Grounding smell.
   a. Identify a scent you really like that is not connected to your trauma.
   b. Obtain a small item that carries this scent, for example, a small lavender sachet or a tissue impregnated with an aromatherapy oil that you like, a small bottle of your favorite perfume or the smell of cedar or cooking vanilla.
   c. Each time you notice the first signs of a flashback breathe in some of this scent and allow yourself to be calmed by it.

3 Grounding object.
   a. Instead of using scent, find a small object, like a stone, a piece of smooth wood, a conker or an acorn or other nut, or a worry stone or worry beads.
   b. Carry this on you and feel, touch and look at it each time you notice the first signs of a flashback.

continued on next page

---

4 Grounding position.
  a. Identify a bodily position that is especially comforting to you. This could be curling up, leaning against a wall, squatting down, etc.
  b. Use this at times when you notice the first signs of a flashback. As these positions can be very personal, you may find they work best when you are on your own.

5 Other techniques that might help ground you during a flashback are simply walking about, telling yourself (silently) your name, the date and time of the day, or reciting a poem or singing a song, or simply squeezing thumb and third finger together.

6 Breathing and relaxation techniques are also very helpful in combination with the exercises suggested here. You will find more information about these in Chapter 8.

Step 3: Flashbacks in Sexual Relationships

For people whose trauma has included abuse of a sexual nature it is common to suffer flashbacks during acts of sexual intimacy. Here are some suggested ways of dealing with these (Dolan, 1991):

1 As soon as you become aware of a flashback, open your eyes (if closed) and focus on the immediate environment around you. Notice where you are.
2 Recognize the differences between your present partner and the perpetrator, between your present environment and that recalled in your flashback.
3 Focus on an object of safety, security or comfort, for example, cuddle the pillow, imagine a pleasant image, use relaxation or any of the grounding techniques suggested above.
4 If the image persists, imagine putting it on a television screen. You have the remote control, you can darken the picture, you can turn off the sound, you can freeze the picture, or you can switch off the TV.

5 Let your partner know what has happened and allow him/her to comfort you if he/she can.
6 Agree beforehand on reassuring things your partner can do or say if this happens.
7 Stop any form of sexual contact until the flashback is completely over.

Recognizing Your Achievements

Congratulations on tackling your intrusive and re-experiencing symptoms. Keep telling yourself that flashbacks and intrusive memories are very common. They are your body's way of trying to make sense of your experiences. The more you allow yourself to get to know them and understand them, the more you will be able to master them and feel in control.

Recognize your achievements and monitor your progress periodically by re-scoring yourself on the scale that appears at the beginning of this chapter. Compare your new score to your old baseline score to find out if there any changes.

8

Managing Your Arousal Reactions

As we discussed earlier, in Chapter 2, a dramatically increased feeling of *arousal* is a major component of the traumatic stress reaction pattern. We described it as the body's alarm system getting stuck on 'red alert', and overreacting to nearly everything. If you have been experiencing high arousal reactions, you will be only too aware of the effects: being constantly aroused interferes with everyday functioning, especially in terms of sleep, temper, jumpiness, nervousness, watchfulness, and a driving need to control everything.

Monitoring Your Arousal Level

It will help if you keep an arousal chart, to gather data on how frequently and how severely these reactions are being triggered for you. In your notebook, make an entry whenever you are startled, snappy, shaky, have an outburst of anger or irritability or experience poor sleep. Describe your reactions quite specifically, according to the 4-point scale we have used in Chapter 7 (see page 67).

The following questions cover the range of commonly experienced arousal reactions. Please copy these questions into your notebook, date the entry and try to answer them as best as you can. The scales 0–3 are explained below:

- To rate how frequently you have had each of the experiences over the past week, use the following 0–3 scale:

```
O            1              2              3
●————————————————————————————————————————————————●
Not at all  Once a week/   2–4 times per week/  5 times per week/
            A little bit/   Somewhat/           Very much/
            Once in a while  Half the time       Almost always
```

* To rate how upsetting each of the experiences has been in the past week, use the following 0–3 scale.

```
O            1              2              3
●————————————————————————————————————————————————●
Not at all                              Very upsetting
upsetting
```

Please answer the following questions by circling the number on each scale which best applies to you:

1 In the past 7 days have you had poor quality sleep, either finding difficulty falling asleep or staying asleep?

   How frequently? 0 1 2 3   How upsetting has this been? 0 1 2 3

2 In the past 7 days have you noticed yourself having flashes of anger or being easily irritated, quick-tempered or argumentative?

   How frequently? 0 1 2 3   How upsetting has this been? 0 1 2 3

3 In the past 7 days have you experienced poor concentration or problems with your memory, such as forgetting things, losing your bearings, having difficulties reading or listening to conversations?

   How frequently? 0 1 2 3   How upsetting has this been? 0 1 2 3

4 In the past 7 days have you been overly watchful or experienced a heightened concern for the safety of yourself or others?

   How frequently? 0 1 2 3   How upsetting has this been? 0 1 2 3

5 In the past 7 days have you felt more on edge, very jumpy or easily startled?

   How frequently? 0 1 2 3   How upsetting has this been? 0 1 2 3

Once you have circled the number that best applies to you on each question, both on the frequency and the upset ratings, add the scores from all the questions (1–5) for each of the two categories. Record these total scores in your notebook.

AROUSAL REACTIONS ON .... (date)

Your total score for
frequency is: ....   If your total scores
                                           on both measures are:
                                           5 or below = they are low
Your total score for   5 – 10 = they fall into
upset is: ....   the mid-range
                                           10 or more = they are high

---

Lastly, give an overall rating for how disabling these arousal reactions have been to you in the past week, by circling the number that applies to you on the scale used below (you could also copy this into your notebook):

0	1	2	3	4	5	6	7	8
Not at all disabling		Slightly disabling		Definitely disabling		Markedly disabling		Severely disabling

Now that you have established your own level of arousal reactions you can begin to try to reduce both the frequency and the level of upset of these. If your scores are high you may benefit from professional help in addition to reading this book.

Improving Your Sleep

Since sleep is so vitally important to a person's mood and reactions, our first step is to improve the quality of your sleep. Here are some strategies to help you get a better night's sleep:

Exercise 10: Improving your sleeping environment

Protecting your sleeping space
Ensure that the doors and windows of your home have proper locks, and if in doubt invest in new ones. You need to feel that your sleeping space is protected as much as possible from external intruders. If your trauma has resulted from a house break-in or a sexual assault, you may need to consider moving house if you cannot feel at ease where you are living now.

If you need to sleep alone for a while (because of restlessness or crying out during sleep), or need to get up and be alone during the night, discuss this ahead of time with your partner. Explain that this will only be temporary because it is part of your recovery process and that it must not be understood as a rejection.

Coping with internal intrusions
To help with 'internal intrusions' in your sleeping environment, such as difficulty falling asleep, nightmares, waking in the night, try the following:

- changing the position of your bed
- rearranging the bedroom layout, using extra pillows as comforting 'props' to hold or bolster you in bed
- removing wall hangings or posters that may appear scary when you are half-awake in a darkened room
- using a night-light
- removing any upsetting reminders (e.g. photographs of life before your trauma)

If flashbacks occur while you are in bed, imagine that you are seeing the images on a video screen. You, as the viewer, have the remote control and can freeze the images, turn off the sound and grey out or fuzz the screen.

continued on next page

Taking care of your body
Avoid alcohol, caffeine or other stimulants before bedtime. Caffeine can be found in coffee, black tea, cocoa or cola drinks, and although you may feel that alcohol relaxes you, it actually has a detrimental effect on sleeping patterns. Do not eat highly spiced or sugary foods late in the evening. Also avoid watching violent television programs or reading disturbing books before bedtime.

Establishing a night-time routine
Establish a regular night-time routine, for example, taking a soothing beverage or a herbal tea, such as chamomile tea. Try and keep to a fairly regular bedtime. Use some easy reading material to help you wind down when you lie in bed. Tapes with relaxing music or relaxation exercises or sounds may also help you to calm down. The **Relaxed Breathing Method** described on page 94 or visualizing a scene that has a peaceful and calming meaning for you, may also help you fall asleep.

To help you get into a positive mind-set before sleep, do a mental 'gratitude journal' (Breathnach, 1995) at the end of each day, as you are getting into bed. Identify 5 things (big or very small) that you are grateful for from the day. These could be very simple – you might be grateful that on that day you spotted the first snowdrops or you heard a very beautiful piece of music on the radio.

Coping with disturbing dreams
Some people dread falling asleep because of disturbing or repetitive dreams and they don't respond well to relaxation techniques used at bedtime, as they fear 'losing control' by letting their guard down and becoming too relaxed. If this applies to you, instead of the relaxation exercises, you might find it helpful to construct a different, more positive ending for a repetitive dream. First, think of a dream that disturbs

continued on next page

you and then try to think of a different ending for it. Concentrate on this by rehearsing it mentally several times before going to sleep.

Alternatively, you could prepare yourself to 'talk back' in your dreams. Imagine ahead of time what you would like to say if that dream occurs and practise it before your bedtime. Say it aloud several times and then imagine saying it to yourself quietly.

You can prepare yourself to cope with bad dreams by reorienting yourself as soon as possible upon awakening. Keep a damp flannel or towel and a bowl of cool water beside the bed for washing your face if you wake up distressed or in a sweat. Mentally rehearse waking up and getting reoriented to the present. Turn the light on, replace your digital clock with a standard analog clock, as the action of 'telling the time' will help you to shift into wakefulness.

Remember: you *can* exert some control over your dreams, especially with practice!

Keep a pad of paper and a pencil by your bed (or couch, if you are falling asleep there) within easy reach. If you want to record your dreams, you can do so without having to sit up and become fully awake, which often causes you to forget details. However, be cautious not to read too much into the meaning of your dreams. They may give you clues to your progress but it might not be helpful to take them too literally. If disturbing themes recur, you might wish to discuss these with a health care professional.

Further strategies

1 Introduce pleasant smells, e.g. potpourri, vanilla, or other scents (but not those associated with your trauma) into your sleeping environment to create a restful atmosphere. Certain aromatherapy oils, such as lavender oil or other such preparations, may help to relax you. You might want

continued on next page

to consult a qualified aromatherapist or you could get yourself a good self-help book on aromatherapy.

2 Physical exercise, during late afternoon or early evening, may also help to enhance sleep. Make sure you allow yourself some time after the exercise to wind down and then go to bed. Alternatively, you might try taking a warm or cool bath, possibly with relaxing bath essences or herbs, before you go to bed. Some people find a hot water bottle very soothing.

3 Remember: If you can't get yourself back to sleep within 30 minutes of going to bed, make sure to get up again and do another activity elsewhere, such as reading a magazine or watching TV. After 15 minutes, go to bed again and try to get to sleep. If you still can't fall asleep, get up again and do another activity. Repeat this process as long as necessary and only use your bed for sleeping in. Do not take a nap during the day, even if you are tired!

4 Medications for sleep may be helpful on a short-term basis, but should always be prescribed and monitored by a qualified medical practitioner. Alternatives such as herbal remedies, homeopathy, massage, aromatherapy or certain forms of relaxation or meditation may be very beneficial, too. You may also benefit if you consult a recognized and well-qualified alternative health practitioner, such as a homeopath or aromatherapist, for advice.

Record in your notebook any other strategies that you discover to be helpful.

Every person is different and it is quite likely that you will need to try out a variety of strategies and alter and change them until you have found the right one for you. It is important to persevere until you have found the most effective method.

In order to find out if your strategies are helping to improve your sleep, use a sleeping log, like the one in Exercise 11.

Exercise 11: Keeping a sleeping log

Copy this log into your notebook or onto your computer. Use it every day during your sleep-monitoring period and remember to fill it out about 15–20 minutes after waking.

Day	Bedtime routine used:	Before I went to sleep I felt (indicate score by circling one from 1 = very tense to 5 = very relaxed)	I went to sleep at time:	During the night I woke at (time):	Action taken to get back to sleep:	I stayed awake for (minutes/ hours):	This morning I woke at:	When I woke up, I felt (indicate score by circling one from 1 = not rested at all to 5 = well-rested):	The following helped me with my sleep last night:
Monday		1 2 3 4 5						1 2 3 4 5	
Tuesday		1 2 3 4 5						1 2 3 4 5	
Wednesday		1 2 3 4 5						1 2 3 4 5	
Thursday		1 2 3 4 5						1 2 3 4 5	
Friday		1 2 3 4 5						1 2 3 4 5	
Saturday		1 2 3 4 5						1 2 3 4 5	
Sunday		1 2 3 4 5						1 2 3 4 5	

Notice those strategies which seem to be helpful and those that don't have a positive effect on your sleep. Discard the unhelpful ones and keep the helpful strategies. In this way, build up your own individualized sleep restoration program.

Relaxed Breathing Method

The following **Relaxed Breathing Method** can be used to lessen tension, promote deeper sleep, or generally to help you relax and regain control when you have been overreacting. Try to learn the method, maybe getting someone to read the instructions to you, so you can concentrate on your breathing. Alternatively, you could record these instructions on tape and play them back whenever you wish. When you first practise this method, use it during times when you don't feel too tense. With practise, the deep breathing method will become much more automatic and then you will also be able to use this method to calm you down.

Exercise 12: Relaxed Breathing Method

When you are anxious or stressed your breathing becomes shallow and you tend to breathe into your upper chest. When this happens, your body is not supplied with sufficient oxygen. Your automatic response to this will often be to breathe even faster, because it feels to you as if you are not getting enough oxygen. However, the faster you breathe and the more oxygen you take in the dizzier and fainter you will feel. This will make you feel less able to function calmly.

In order for you to gain the optimum benefit from your breathing, it should be *deep*, so that your stomach wall pushes IN as you breathe out, and OUT as you breathe in. This type of deep breathing helps your body to relax and, if used systematically, can make you feel calm and refreshed. The following steps describe how you can achieve such relaxed breathing. You can practise this as often during the day or night as you like. The more you practise, the sooner you will be able to use this exercise wherever you are and whenever you feel a little tense. To start with you

continued on next page

---

might not achieve the desired effect Don't worry about this and you will soon find that relaxation will be achieved with regular practice.

1 First of all, stop whatever you are doing and concentrate on giving this time to yourself. Tell yourself that nothing else is important at the moment, and that everything can be put to one side for a while, until you feel more refreshed. Ensure that others will not disturb you during this time.

2 Find a comfortable chair to sit in or lie down on the floor and loosen any tight clothing. Start by stretching and then try to make yourself as comfortable as you possibly can. Keep your arms by your side and keep them as relaxed as possible. You may wish to close your eyes since this will help you to concentrate better.

3 Now just sit or lie like this for a while and concentrate on your breathing. Feel your breath going in and out of your body and just stay with it for a while. Don't try to force it, just breathe naturally. See if you can feel the rhythm of your breathing as you breathe in and out. Also notice whether your breath feels warm or cold and keep concentrating on this for a while.

4 When you feel ready, gently put your hands onto your stomach. Now see if you can feel your breath going in and out of your stomach; lifting your hands up as you breathe in and lowering them as you breathe out. Try and concentrate just on your breathing, making sure that you breathe slowly and evenly. Just feel the gentle massaging action of your breath on the muscles inside of your stomach wall.

5 Now take in a deep breath and feel your stomach wall rising. Hold it there for a few seconds and then let go, feeling your stomach contracting as you slowly breathe out. Then do the same again and this time, as you

continued on next page

breathe out, think of the word 'relax'. Take one or two more deep breaths and each time, as you slowly breathe out, think of the word 'relax'. You may also think of your favorite calm color, a peaceful image or relaxing music as you breathe out. In your own time return to breathing normally, but still think of the word 'relax', color and/or image and/or sound as you breathe out. Feel a sense of calmness spreading all over your body as your stomach muscles slowly go up and down with each breath.

6 You can now take your hands off your stomach if you wish, but still continue to breathe slowly and evenly into your stomach. Just stay with the rhythm of your breathing for as long as you can, relaxing more and more with every breath out.

7 When you are ready, in your own time, count forward mentally, from one to five, becoming gradually more alert, and then slowly open your eyes. Stay seated or lying down for a little while longer and feel how relaxed and refreshed you have become. When you get up, make sure to rise slowly and take some time before getting back to your normal activities.

Managing Your Anger

Another common traumatic stress arousal reaction is an increased feeling of anger. This may range from general irritability to a deep-seated, explosive rage. You might find yourself arguing with your family or co-workers over unimportant things or carrying a smoldering hatred toward individuals or larger groups that you hold responsible for your misfortune. This type of anger reaction may remain extremely intense, lasting months or years, and will probably affect your relationships with others.

While your angry feelings may be quite justified, how you manage and express them is important, both to your own well-being and healing as well as to your sense of effectiveness and control. Working on your anger management skills is a positive step towards eliminating the risk of violent behavior. This ensures the safety of yourself, your family and others and generally helps you to resolve conflict constructively, without alienating others.

It's very understandable that you want to blame others for what has happened to you, particularly if the situation could have been prevented or improved by other people's actions. You will probably find, too, that your feelings of blame consist of a confusing mixture of guilt, fear, shame, loss of faith in a just society and your own sense of personal vulnerability.

When you have been traumatized, the source of your anger may also be linked with feeling a lack of control over situations, which you may not have experienced before. The same physical arousal symptoms – a pounding heart, sweating palms, rapid breathing, rising blood pressure – that are present during a situation of tremendous stress or fear are experienced when anger is 'on the boil'. Suppressing this chronic anger response has been linked to health problems for both men and women, manifesting in heart attacks, high blood pressure and severe headaches.

Nevertheless, in some instances anger can be useful! For example, when it leads to a struggle against injustice, when it helps a parent to defend a child or when it leads to community action on a problem. Properly handled, it can help you to achieve better, more honest communication through talking rather than shouting. The key is to channel your anger effectively. For example, getting a legal representative to pursue a claim on your behalf allows that person to be angry for you, in an appropriate way, so that you can let go of some of the anger and deal with other everyday matters.

On the other hand, when anger is bottled up until it explodes, the results can be dangerous and violent. Many people who have been wronged have revenge fantasies. They imagine horrible punishments for those that they hold responsible for their tragedy. While it's not uncommon to have such thoughts, it is important to distinguish between fantasy (what you think about) and reality (what you actually do). While a revenge fantasy may act as a useful release at times, to dwell upon it and to consider taking violent action puts you at risk, as well as the other party. Acting out your rage will not erase what has happened, and it could result in serious consequences for you!

The people who seem to fare best are those who learn how to understand their own tempers, and express their anger appropriately. By achieving a healthy distance, they are able to move on with their lives, instead of remaining victims of their experience.

Rather than feeling 'stuck' in an anger arousal cycle, where every little thing that happens triggers the same overly angry response and you seem to be either suppressing it or lashing out at others, taking responsibility for managing your own anger is a positive step towards gaining control over your life again. When you are able to manage your anger effectively, you will have more choices about how you respond in any given situation.

Techniques for Anger Management

In this section, you will be asked to work on three steps through the proposed exercises. Each exercise contains at least two parts.

- Step 1 will be to keep your own notes and to ask yourself specific questions, in order to understand your anger and therefore gain more control over it.
- Step 2 will teach you to work with your own body, to notice the signs of tension building up in your muscles, as well as the signs of fatigue or stress that may make you susceptible to a temper outburst. Your goal is to be better able to predict when you are at risk of losing control and of becoming aggressive with others (or even with yourself).
- In Step 3 you will be introduced to some anger management techniques. Try these techniques, at least a few times each: the 'Time-Out', the 'Thermometer Technique' and the 'Assertive Exchange' – and find the ones that work best for you.

Exercise 13: Step 1– Keeping your own anger notes

Part 1: Set aside a section in your notebook and label it 'Anger Notes'. Draw five vertical columns and in these keep track of:

1 when you get angry
2 what's happened to cause the anger
3 how strong it feels (give it a rating between 0–8, see below)
4 how you think and
5 how you behave when you are angry.

For example, your thoughts might be: 'I can't stand this!', 'I'll get even for that!', 'They're driving me crazy', 'I can't believe what I'm hearing!' Your behavior might include making sarcastic remarks, shouting, slamming doors, throwing something, swearing, ignoring others or trying to over-control them.

Use the following scale 0–8 to rate the strength of your anger:

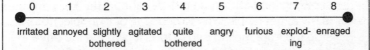

0	1	2	3	4	5	6	7	8
irritated	annoyed	slightly bothered	agitated	quite bothered	angry	furious	exploding	enraged

In your notebook you should make entries at least once daily for a period of two weeks or more. Remember that, just like the rest of your notebook, these notes are for your own reference and for your eyes alone – so you can be completely honest with yourself!

It is hard to remember things clearly when one is in the heat of anger. Keeping the notes will give you a chance to look back a few days or weeks later and decide if you are managing your anger effectively or if some things still need improvement. Even if you are not a person who usually

continued on next page

writes things down, or even if you are uncomfortable doing so, do make an effort to do this. You will not remember accurately otherwise, and you may even find that the act of writing itself gives your arousal reactions time to CALM DOWN.

Part 2 of Exercise 13 offers some very specific questions to ask yourself in order to help you understand your anger even better.

Exercise 13: Step 1 – Keeping your own anger notes

Part 2: Ask yourself the following questions and record the answers in your notebook as part of your anger notes as honestly as you can:

1   How often do I feel angry? (Three times a day/every other day/once a week?)
2   How do I let others know that I'm angry? (By shouting/by being silent/are others even aware/do I keep it hidden?)
3   What do I look like when I'm angry? (Red in the face/ scowling/face muscles tight/clenched fists?)
4   Is my anger helping me to cope? (For example, does it stop me from feeling sad? Does it give me the drive to deal with legal matters, bank managers, etc.?)
5   Is my anger getting in the way of my recovery? (For example, does it help me to avoid other things that I need to face? Does it alienate me from my family?)
6   What do I hope to gain from my anger? (Confidence/ restitution/ recognition/ revenge?)
7   Are there other ways in which I could gain those things?
8   What is my anger preventing me from doing? (For example, talking to others, forming new relationships, gaining some distance from the trauma?)
9   Is feeling angry different from feeling powerful? (Yes *or* no) If the answer is 'yes', how is it different?

continued on next page

10 In what situations do I feel powerful?

11 How did people in my family express anger while I was growing up?

12 Do I use the same ways? If not, how are the ways I use different?

13 How have my ways of handling anger changed since the trauma ?(For example, do I throw things now, when I didn't before? Do I shout at the children more?)

14 Have I been hoping to obtain some relief from angry, explosive actions? (Yes *or* no) If the answer is 'yes', is this a fantasy or a realistic expectation?

15 What other more helpful methods could I use to obtain relief?

16 Do I feel or behave like a victim? (Yes *or* no) If the answer is 'yes', is that helpful to me now?

17 Is it better to 'forgive and forget' or to seek revenge? Are there any alternatives that lie in between those two extremes?

18 Add any other questions of your own here that you might find useful to ask.

Keep working on your anger notes, make entries daily, so that you can keep track of your feelings and how you are managing your anger in different situations. Try and see if you can recognize a pattern. Write down the date, what it was about the situation that made you angry, and the bodily behavior signals that told you that you were angry, for example: changes in your breathing, muscles tight in forehead, tightness in your chest or stomach, gritting your teeth, clenched fists, raised voice, pacing, making sarcastic comments. The 'signals' will probably differ with different levels of intensity of your anger. Try to see if you can recognize a pattern in your responses.

Don't expect that this exercise will go perfectly. Your anger notes are intended to help you to observe your own ways of dealing with things, and to become familiar with your individual physical and behavioral signals for different levels of anger. Step 2 continues this process.

Exercise 14: Step 2 – Managing your physical self

Part 1: To understand your own body, ask yourself the following questions and record the answers in your notebook:

1 How does your body tell you that you are becoming angry?
2 How do you recognize the signals?
3 Does your stomach go into a knot?
4 Do your muscles become tense and stiff?
5 Do you start to sweat or get cold?
6 Does your head begin to pound?
7 Do you feel veins standing out in your neck or forehead?
8 What other signals have you noticed for your anger?

It will be helpful for you to get to know your body and your physical responses as best as you can. Many of the physical signs of anger are similar to the anxiety responses described in Chapter 2 (see page 15). In fact, unexpressed anger may often be masked as anxiety.

The **Relaxed Breathing Method** that you read about earlier in this chapter will also be useful to help you to reduce your tension and to gain control over your body's responses to anger. When you have mastered your technique, you can begin to employ **Quick Controlled Breathing**, which is described below, to help you in situations of high arousal.

Exercise 14: Step 2 – Managing your physical self

Part 2: Control your body's responses to anger with the **Quick Controlled Breathing** technique

1 Pay attention to your breathing when you feel yourself becoming angry. Is it sharper? Faster? Can you slow it down by taking five deep breaths?

continued on next page

---

2 Start by exhaling as fully as you can. Now with each breath, inhale, hold for a second, then exhale slowly, blowing through your mouth. Again, with each breath, inhale, hold for a second, then exhale slowly, blowing through your mouth and counting (silently) backwards from 5 to 1.

3 Remember to exhale fully, as if it was a heavy sigh, then again inhale, hold, exhale slowly, counting 5,4,3,2,1. Next breath, inhale, hold, exhale slowly, counting 5,4,3,2,1.

4 Continue three more times and on the last breath say softly to yourself: 'Calm and in control'.

5 As you perform this you should notice a slight drop in your angry feelings. This will help you to think more clearly, so that you can choose how to react. Practise this technique frequently!

In addition to using relaxed breathing, try some healthy physical outlets for your tension, for example, a competitive sport, a vigorous walk or a run, or even enthusiastic house-repair, cleaning or redecorating. Physical exertion, in the form of exercise or physical activity, is a good outlet for anger and stress. If the traditional types of sport and exercise do not appeal to you, consider some of the less traditional, like the martial arts, Tai Chi or yoga. Bowling, swimming or cycling are other possibilities.

One activity it is best to avoid when you are in a temper is *driving*. Instead, a vigorous walk is a good way to calm you down. Make sure you don't engage in activities where you could hurt yourself or others, for example, pounding nails with a hammer when angry often results in smashed thumbnails. Throwing hard or breakable objects is also off-limits. Instead, pound a pillow, bounce a soft ball or even blow up balloons (balloons require effort and vigorous breathing, another form of breathing control, so this is not as silly as it sounds!).

Remember to keep track in your notebook of what you do and how often, and whether it makes a difference in the way you feel.

Exercise 15: Step 3 – Specific anger management techniques

Part 1: The 'Time-out' technique

Perhaps the most successful and widely used method for gaining control over an explosive temper is known as 'Time-out'. It is particularly useful for traumatized individuals, as it allows them to be 'in charge' of their own anger, paying attention to the body signals of rising frustration and *choosing,* before they lose control, to take a 'Time-out'. 'Time-out' means leaving the situation so that your anger will not escalate.

If you are at home at the time you feel your anger rising, say out loud to yourself and your partner: 'I'm getting angry and I need to take a "Time-out".' Then, you must *leave* for an hour (no more and no less), during which time you must not drink alcohol and you should not drive.

If it is late at night, and unsafe to go out, go to another room and remain alone.

Use the breathing technique or any other techniques, such as physical exercise, to help you calm down. This will help you to deal with things on your return, rather than just reacting to them in an 'out-of-control' way.

Prior preparation

Before you first use this technique, it is important to explain to your partner or others around you that may be affected, that you are trying to learn helpful ways of controlling your anger. Make an agreement with them beforehand that when you are next angry you will take a 'Time-out', but that you will be back after an hour and that they should not worry because you will take good care of yourself during that time. Also explain that your going away does not mean you don't want to be with them, but that there are times when you need to be alone in order to cope better with

continued on next page

your anger. Encourage them to respect your efforts at anger control and ask them to give you the freedom to use this technique without stopping you or coming after you when you feel angry, as this would not be helpful.

Exercise 15: Step 3 – Specific anger management techniques

Part 2: The 'Thermometer' technique

This approach draws on your newly developed skills of paying attention to your bodily signals, in particular, signs of temper rising. It has been taught (in various forms) and used successfully for many years by groups such as Narcotics Anonymous, whose participants have often turned to drug or alcohol abuse as an ineffective way of managing explosive tempers. When people are working to overcome addictions, they often feel quite raw and on edge, just as you are likely to be feeling at times, while you work to overcome the effects of traumatic stress.

Here is how it works:

1 Picture, in your mind's eye, a very large thermometer. Try and allow yourself to see very clearly the gradation marks on each side of the glass tube that register the degrees of temperature rising. The mercury inside the glass tube is red. We will use this to represent your temper.
2 When you are calm and cool, there is very little mercury in the tube, just enough to help you pay attention and interact effectively with others. However, when you start to become agitated, the temperature starts to rise and the mercury level in the tube will go up!

continued on next page

3   Because you are much more in tune with your bodily signals now, you will notice how your breathing begins to quicken when you become just a bit agitated. Your muscles tense, and you become aware that your eyes are squinting a bit, your nostrils are flaring. In short, as your 'temperature rises', you are starting to resemble a charging bull! The mercury in your imaginary thermometer is rising very quickly indeed.

4   Now, all thermometers have some red marks at the top to indicate 'danger' and 'overheating'. As you pay attention to the signals of your rising anger, you can start to picture the thermometer, and you can become aware of how close you are getting to the danger zone. It is time to bring the mercury down before you get into the 'red zone', where you will not be able to think clearly enough to take appropriate action.

5   If you allow your anger to boil over, you will be operating on raw emotion, with very little (if any) rational thought. Those are the situations where you are likely to get into trouble and do or say things that you will probably regret later, when they are hard to undo. Use all your skills to stay out of the red zone of raw emotions.

6   Keep being aware of your temper. Try using the 'Quick Controlled Breathing' technique described above. Take a step back and let the intensity of your voice drop. Wait a few moments, take a 'Time-out' if you need to. Do whatever you need to do to get your anger 'thermometer' to drop the temperature down to a more reasonable and comfortable level.

7   When you have reached 'room temperature' level again, then you can begin to deal with the person or problem on a rational basis.

Practise this technique as often as possible. As soon as you find yourself getting worked up, think 'THERMOMETER'! This technique can be very effective, once you have learned it and as long as you use it regularly.

Exercise 15: Step 3 – Specific anger management techniques

Part 3: The 'Assertive Exchange' technique

When you have some mastery over the surges that fuel your temper, the next skill to work on is improving your communication. If the only way you communicate when you are frustrated or angry is to be sarcastic, intimidating, shouting, aggressive, blaming or giving the silent 'freeze treatment', your partner, family members or colleagues are unlikely to want to engage in problem-solving with you! They know you are angry, but they probably stop listening at an early stage and are busy thinking about how to defend themselves. Nothing gets resolved, and the situation tends to repeat itself in a vicious and very frustrating circle.

You can change this by developing your assertiveness skills.

The following technique, which we call the 'Assertive Exchange', is based on the work of Sharon Anthony Bower and Gordon Bower, who outlined a method called the D-E-S-C script in their 1976 book Asserting Yourself. It has become the basis for most assertiveness communication training.

An easy way to remember our 'Assertive Exchange' formula is to think of the acronym, **'R-E-A-C-T'**, which stands for:

Refer: state directly the issue that is upsetting you and that you want to talk about.
   Example: *'James, the television is turned up too loud!'*

Exchange: use an 'I' statement here to communicate your feelings.
   Example: *'I've spoken to you about this several times already. I'm frustrated that you're not listening.'*

Action: be specific about the action you want to take place; what is it that you want the person to do?
   Example: *'Turn the television down immediately.'*

continued on next page

Conditions: if appropriate, now indicate any stipulations or
consequences.
  Example: *'This is the last time I'm going to speak to
  you about it.'*

Thanks: express gratitude to the other person for listening.
  Example: *'Thank you. I appreciate you turning it down'*

This very simple method may feel like a big leap for you,
but it is fairly certain to produce positive results, both at
home and in the outside world. It works with children,
partners, co-workers, and even most bosses and authority
figures!

Why is it so effective? Because it emphasizes fact, and
it keeps emotion in check. It does not focus on the blaming
'you' statement (e.g. 'You make me sick!'), which is more
aggressive and puts the other person on the defensive.
That is the difference between aggressiveness and
assertiveness. When you are being properly assertive, more
respect is communicated between the parties and emotions
tend to stay in check. The result is that you stay in control
and more problem-solving happens. By using this
technique, you may begin to feel more understood and more
effective in achieving the result that you need.

If you have a difficult exchange coming up, where you need to
stay assertive and not explode with frustration, apply this R-E-A-
C-T formula in a rehearsal before the encounter takes place.
Write out each step of what you are going to say in your notebook. Imagine how the other person may respond and visualize
yourself staying on track. This imaginary rehearsal will greatly
enhance your chances for success!

Final Comments on Anger Reactions

In moments of extreme frustration – especially as one is struggling to overcome a trauma, and one feels very helpless to do
anything else – it is tempting to take it out on yourself. Banging

one's head, putting a fist through the wall or window, driving recklessly, cutting or self-mutilating are all examples of behavior that says that you have lost control.

This type of behavior is a sure sign that you are not coping, and that things have become too much for you. In this case, *you should seek the help of a professional*. Remove yourself from the situation and away from the people who are causing you to want to harm yourself. Remind yourself that such behavior is a desperate bid for control and, as you have seen in this chapter, there are better ways to achieve control.

9

Managing Your Avoidance And Numbing Reactions

Getting to Know Your Avoidance Reactions

In order to be able to manage your avoidance reactions, you also need to know how frequent and how upsetting to you they are. Measuring the frequency and the level of upset of your reactions will enable you to take your *avoidance baseline* (just as you did in Chapter 7 for your intrusive reactions).

The following questions cover the range of commonly experienced avoidance reactions. Please copy these questions into your notebook, date the entry and try to answer them as best as you can. The scales 0–3 are explained below:

- To rate how frequently you have had each of the experiences over the past week, use the following 0–3 scale:

0	1	2	3
Not at all	Once a week/ A little bit/ Once in a while	2–4 times per week/ Somewhat/ Half the time	5 times per week/ Very much/ Almost always

- To rate how upsetting each of the experiences has been in the past week, use the following 0–3 scale.

0	1	2	3
Not at all upsetting	Quite upsetting	Very upsetting	Extremely upsetting

Please answer the following questions by circling the number on each scale which best applies to you:

Managing Your Avoidance and Numbing Reactions

1 In the past 7 days have you tried to push out of your mind any thoughts, pictures or feelings that reminded you of your traumatic experience?

How frequently? o 1 2 3   How upsetting has this been? o 1 2 3

2 In the past 7 days have you not done or stayed away from activities, situations or places which reminded you of your traumatic experience (including conversations with others)?

How frequently? o 1 2 3   How upsetting has this been? o 1 2 3

3 In the past 7 days have there been any important aspects of your traumatic experience that you have tried to remember but have been unable to?

How frequently? o 1 2 3   How upsetting has this been? o 1 2 3

4 In the past 7 days have you been less motivated or interested or just couldn't be bothered to do things or activities that you used to enjoy?

How frequently? o 1 2 3   How upsetting has this been? o 1 2 3

5 In the past 7 days have you felt cut off and detached from people in your surroundings?

How frequently? o 1 2 3   How upsetting has this been? o 1 2 3

6 In the past 7 days have you experienced yourself as emotionally shut-down or numb or been unable to respond emotionally when you knew you should, for example losing your sense of humour, being unable to respond to affection or to the feelings of others, etc.?

How frequently? o 1 2 3   How upsetting has this been? o 1 2 3

7 In the past 7 days have you been unable to think about yourself as having a future or been unable to make plans or decisions concerning your life?

How frequently? o 1 2 3   How upsetting has this been? o 1 2 3

Once you have circled the number that best applies to you on each question, both on the frequency and the upset ratings, add the total scores from all the questions (1–7) for each of the two categories. Record these total scores in your notebook.

AVOIDANCE REACTIONS ON .... (date)

Your total score for
frequency is: ....

Your total score for
upset is: ....

If your total scores
on both measures are:
7 or below = they are low
7 – 14 = they fall into
the mid-range
14 or more = they are high

Lastly, give an overall rating for how disabling these avoidance reactions have been to you in the past week, by circling the number that applies to you on the scale used below (you might try and copy this also into your notebook):

0	1	2	3	4	5	6	7	8
Not at all disabling		Slightly disabling		Definitely disabling		Markedly disabling		Severely disabling

Now that you have established your own avoidance reactions you can begin to try to reduce both the frequency and the upset level of these. You may also find that professional help would be useful if your scores fall into the high range.

The Avoidance – Panic Connection

Although panic reactions are really rooted in responses of heightened arousal, such as anxiety and fear, we have chosen to discuss them in this chapter because they are so directly linked to avoidance behavior.

If you have ever experienced a panic attack, the sudden shortness of breath, severe chest pain or feeling that your head was expanding may have led you to wonder if you had a serious illness or were going mad. The feelings are so dreadful that immediately you begin to worry about this happening to you again and as a result you are 'on the look-out' for the slightest signs of increasing nervousness within yourself. In order to reduce the chances of a recurrence, you might begin *to avoid* situations, places, and activities that you think are likely to make you feel uncomfortable or uneasy, and bring on a panic attack. The cycle of anxiety leading to avoidance leading to the anticipation of more anxiety leading to more avoidance has begun.

Coping with Panic and Avoidance

Francis Charlton, a trauma therapist, states in his (1992) pamphlet, 'Coping With Panics', that '...the greatest part of what makes up a panic is that your thoughts get out of hand and run away with you!' He goes on to say, 'No one can die of fright and panic attacks cannot send you mad, although temporarily you may feel unlike your self. Though panic feelings are unpleasant they cannot in any way harm you, or damage vital organs. The feelings themselves are quite normal. It is just that they are happening in an ordinary situation rather than in a dangerous or frightening one.'

Often these 'ordinary situations' are more public activities, like shopping, or using public transportation. Driving could become a problem as well, if you start to fear that you will have a panic attack while in traffic or on the motorway. You may no longer trust yourself to stay in control, and feel you cannot predict when the anxiety will arise. Thus, you avoid more things, and life becomes more limited.

In order to cope with these panic feelings, and to reduce your fears in anticipation of them, try to tell yourself that you are overreacting in an ordinary situation. As a result of the trauma that you have been through, your body and mind have been conditioned to perceive danger even in situations seemingly unrelated to the traumatic event.

Rather than trying to figure out the cause of the anxiety try to gain confidence in managing those panic reactions. Focus on controlling your breathing, count down slowly from 10 to 1 and congratulate yourself on small successes ('I was able to stay out shopping for half an hour before I began to mind the crowds'). Once you are no longer frightened by them, and give them less attention, the panic attacks will usually disappear on their own.

Exercise 16: Quick tips for handling your panic

1 Remind yourself that you understand what is happening to you now, and that there is no real need to be frightened. Remember these symptoms are uncomfortable but not dangerous!

2 Begin to concentrate on your breathing. Blow out first, as slowly as you can. The next breath in will be deeper. Try to breathe out to the count of 10, then in again to the count of 10, breathing from your diaphragm (belly) and not from the top of your chest.

3 Repeat a coping statement to yourself – 'I can get through this' or 'This feeling will pass in a few seconds if only I stay with it!'.

4 Slow down a bit and continue what you were doing, as calmly as possible. Try not to rush home.

5 If the feelings continue, try singing! If you are alone in the car, while driving, sing out loud and if you are with others, hum a tune or sing softly under your breath. Try to pick a song that makes you feel good, strong, or cheerful!

6 Congratulate yourself on your progress in continuing your trauma recovery program. It is hard work and you are not giving up!

7 When you are in a comfortable place again, practise the **Relaxed Breathing Method** (Chapter 8), and try to let go of the built-up tension.

It will also help if you keep a record in your notebook for a two-week period, noting when you feel panicky or anxious and what was happening at that time. For example, were you in a particular place, or with certain people, or especially tired or upset?

At the same time, make a list of the things you have been avoiding because of the panic attacks and select *one* to work on first. Then decide what *gradual steps* you could take towards resuming that activity. Order them from easiest to hardest, and start work on an easy step first. This should make you feel just a little uncomfortable, but not overwhelmingly so. Record your progress and your successes in your notebook. Use Exercise 17 and the examples below to help you.

Exercise 17: The gradual steps exercise to cope with panic and avoidance

1 Keep a record of your panic attacks in your notebook. Rate them in terms of their strength (using a scale between 0 = none and 8 = absolutely overwhelming) and monitor them on a daily basis.

Here's an example of what your panic diary might look like for a one-week period:

Panic Diary

Time	Sunday	Monday	Tuesday	Wednesday	Thursday	Friday	Saturday
a.m.		Panic = 7					
noon					Panic = 4		
p.m.				Panic = 3			

Notes:
Monday: Went shopping, felt anxious and nauseous, quite strong, therefore I came home.
Wednesday: Had doctor's appointment, tried to go by bus, panicked and took taxi instead.
Thursday: Upset because of an argument at home, panicked while doing the shopping.

continued on next page

---

2 Next, look at the notes in your panic diary and decide on an activity that you have been avoiding, but would now like to try to master again. Choose an activity that won't be too easy but also not completely overwhelming. State precisely what it is that you would be able to achieve if you were to master this target activity. For example, based on the panic diary, below:

Target activity: *'To go on the bus, by myself, when it is crowded, with a reasonable level of comfort.'*

3 Then list the steps (from easiest to hardest) that you have to take to be able to achieve your target activity.

Example list of steps towards that goal:

a. *Decide which bus route is least threatening and most pleasant.*

b. *Walk to the bus stop at a time when it is not crowded, and just wait there for a while. If a bus comes by, don't get on. Leave to go back whenever ready.*

c. *On a day when feeling particularly well, ask a friend to come along for a short bus ride (one or two stops only). Pick a non-crowded time.*

d. *Practise taking short rides alone. If the bus looks too crowded when it arrives, wait for the next one. If I become too uncomfortable, I'll get off at the next stop and wait a little while until I come back on another bus.*

e. *Gradually I will begin to practise getting onto more and more crowded buses. If sometimes this is too hard for me, I have to just get off that time but try again another time, with a slightly less crowded bus.*

f. *The most important aspect of all this is that I persevere and don't give up trying, even when at times I have to take a step backwards rather than forwards.*

g. *The more often I practise the more likely I am to master the target activity!*

The same technique of setting one target at a time, and identifying a series of small, very gradual steps towards a goal will work for any number of feared activities or situations. It is very successful, for example, with driving phobias, which are very common after road traffic accidents.

In the case of a driving phobia, you would also prepare a hierarchy of steps, ranging from easiest to hardest, that you would need to master in order to achieve your target activity. For example, your list might look something like this:

- Open car door and just sit in it (easiest) . (Wait until you feel ready to move to the next step.)
- Turning the key while sitting in the car. (Wait until you feel ready to move to the next step.)
- Put the car into gear and drive a few yards down your road and back (or if your road is really busy, ask your partner or a friend to drive you to a quiet area where you can practise driving a few yards). (Continue practising until you feel comfortable to move to the next step.)
- Drive down the whole of your street and back. (Continue until you feel ready for the next step.)
- Drive round your neighborhood and back. (Continue until you feel ready for the next step.)
- Go for a ten-minute drive in the car, while it is light. (Continue until you feel ready for next step.)
- Go on a drive along a major road to visit a friend (hardest) – and so on.

It would be helpful for you to monitor and record your level of anxiety or panic each time you practise these steps. You should also write down:

- What you used that helped you achieve this practice,
- What was not so helpful about the things you did and
- What, if anything, you would like to do differently during your next practice.

Make sure that you congratulate yourself on the progress you have achieved each time and don't be despondent if progress is slow. Confidence comes through a series of small, but increasing successes.

Coping with Safety Behavior during Driving and Other Activities

When you have been in a trauma that occurred while you were engaged in an activity, like driving, it is more than likely that you will now associate a certain amount of fear with that activity. This might lead you to be extra cautious when you are driving, or doing whatever you were doing at the time of the trauma. Many people start to adopt what are called 'safety behaviors' when they subsequently try those feared activities. For example, if your fear concerns driving, you might now look more frequently in the mirror, get really panicky before a sharp bend, avoid overtaking, use only the slow lane on the motorway, find yourself breaking too frequently and sometimes unnecessarily, only drive during daytime hours, never use busy roads and so on. You might even find yourself behaving in strange ways when you are a passenger in the car. Your partner might find your constant comments about his/her driving irritating, you might scan the road ahead of you very alertly or clasp your seat very tightly, you might even be pressing an imaginary brake pedal while someone else is driving.

This behavior is linked to your panicky feelings and may be so distressing that at times you are tempted to avoid driving or travelling as a passenger altogether. It is important to recognize that such behavior is the body's attempt at protecting itself from something that has in the past been a danger! Your body and mind remember that danger and want to warn you because they think that the danger is still around now. In order to overcome this pattern of behavior you will need to teach yourself that the feared situations are no longer dangerous.

Make a list in your notebook of all the kinds of protective behavior that you find yourself using. Tackle them one by one, telling yourself that you do not need them, even if you feel uncomfortable at times when you do the activity concerned. Try using relaxation and breathing techniques instead and resist these over-anxious responses, which are actually making you less safe.

Managing Emotional Numbness

If you have been feeling emotionally closed off and empty inside, as described in Chapter 2, you should begin to ask yourself (gently): 'What am I trying not to face?'. Often this type of reaction indicates that your mind is trying to protect you from an emotion that you are afraid of, for example: 'I am afraid to love again', 'I am afraid to trust again', or 'I never want to feel that bad again'. In effect, you are hiding from your emotions, for fear they will overtake and destroy you.

It is important for you to take things slowly and not be over-whelmed, as that is likely to cause a setback. Be wary of highly charged emotional situations for this reason. Working slowly and privately – by yourself or with the help of a health care professional – you must begin to acknowledge the parts of your experience that you are trying not to face:

- What has been the meaning of this trauma for you?
- Are you drawing conclusions from it that are inclined to be bitter or cynical and that are keeping you emotionally closed off?
- Have you been trying to justify this behavior to yourself?

Whether you are managing avoidance behavior or other avoid-ance responses, like emotional numbness, the same technique of gradual exposure – taking things bit by bit, one step at a time – should be applied. In all situations, your goal is to achieve containment of your reactions. You have already had your cop-ing abilities overwhelmed by the traumatic experience(s) you have been through. This book aims to help you develop strate-gies to enable you to deal with your reactions without feeling 'wiped out' and experiencing setbacks to your recovery.

If you begin to feel overwhelmed by the work you are doing with this book, it may be a sign that you are trying to do too much too fast or that it is time to talk to a professional. The key is not to be impatient with yourself! Healing rarely occurs in a straight line.

Emotional numbness does not usually go away on its own. You have to challenge it and be willing to examine its origins. Often it is connected to a significant loss that you have experi-enced, perhaps even a sense that you have *lost your identity* through the trauma (Sheehan, 1994). You may have lost your job or your ability to work or your place in a professional group (such as a military unit, or fire fighters' team); part of your identity may have been wrapped up in your plans for the future. Losing the possibility of achieving hopes and dreams or not being able to be the person you hoped to become may have caused you to shut down emotionally.

Exercise 18: Rediscovering your personal identity

Ask yourself the following questions and write your answers to them in your notebook:

1 Who am I now, after the trauma?
2 How do I define myself?
3 What personal expectations did I have before that I no longer think I can achieve?
4 How do I compare myself with others?
5 Have I been treating myself like a 'broken person'?
6 What is it that I am afraid others will see?
7 What is it that I am afraid to admit to myself?

The 'Climbing Chart' exercise, which follows in Chapter 10, may also help you to look at the series of life incidents which helped to shape your sense of personal identity before the trauma hit.

Numbness is often experienced as part of a *grieving response* for a lost loved one, even if that loss has occurred some time ago. To turn feelings back on after they have been turned off completely, feels frightening and sometimes disloyal to the person or people you have lost traumatically. The discussion of grief reactions in Chapter 12 may also help you to recognize these patterns in your own responses and the exercises there will assist you in dealing with your loss more directly, rather than suppressing your feelings by staying numb.

Dependence on Alcohol, Drugs or Comfort Eating

Emotional numbness is one way the unconscious mind responds to overwhelming emotional pain. But that reaction is designed to be short-term, to provide immediate protection to the traumatized person. What often happens is that the conscious mind artificially extends the numbness reaction by the overuse of alcohol, drugs or comfort foods (the severe restriction of food intake, *anorexia nervosa*, may also begin as a reaction to a traumatic experience).

After a trauma, it takes a remarkably brief time for what seemed like a short-term coping strategy to become a dependency, and thus further problems are created. It is therefore essential to confront any substance dependency problems that might have developed if you are to make any headway in reducing your avoidance and numbness reactions.

Try to gauge whether you have a problem with dependency by asking yourself the following questions (and answer as honestly as you can):

1 Am I using any substance – alcohol, drugs, sleep medications, comfort foods, etc. – in a different way than I did before the trauma?
2 What is the difference?
3 How much more am I using of these substances?
4 How much more often am I using them?
5 Do I try to block out pain, fear, anger, sadness or other stressful emotions with the use of substances?
6 Does that work?
7 What price am I paying? What are the side effects of this?
8 Do I now use alcohol, drugs or food to numb emotions in order to sleep?
9 Would I be embarrassed to admit to someone else (like my medical practitioner) how much more I am drinking, or eating, or taking drugs now? (If the answer is 'yes', that is a clear indicator of an overuse problem.)
10 Am I anxious at the prospect of having these substances less available in my life? (Again, a 'yes' indicates dependency problems.)

Substance dependency is often closely linked with the presence of depression. If you recognize your own behavior in the preceding questions, it is very important for your own well-being and healing that you set aside any feelings of embarrassment and talk to someone who can help you with this. Nearly every community, no matter how small, has access to resources for people who are struggling with substance abuse problems. Contact your medical practitioner first and take up any referrals until you have obtained the help you need.

Managing Feelings of Alienation and Problems with Intimacy

If you feel you have lost the capacity to connect to the world and to your loved ones, as a result of the trauma you have experienced, you can feel very lonely and isolated. As a result of your experience the world feels numb, cold and alien – it becomes a place where you survive, but no longer thrive. Whatever the root of your trauma, whatever its deepest meaning, it is truly personal and it may seem impossible for anyone else to even begin to understand how much you've gone through and are still going through.

In your present state of mind it might seem logical to think that to remain alienated from others is the best way to avoid further risk. Such post-traumatic reactive thinking is based on the notions, 'I can never trust again', 'No one will ever understand', 'I will never let anyone get that close to me again' and 'To feel again leaves me open to be hurt again'.

Without a doubt, every time we enter into a trusting or intimate relationship with another human being there is an element of risk. Certain factors and future outcomes are beyond our ability to predict. The fear of loss of control through connection with another person perpetuates a sense of alienation by maintaining a restricted, narrow emotional world.

As before, to reduce avoidance behavior you need to decide on a specific target or goal and to identify a series of very small, gradually increasing steps towards that goal. The coping techniques of the **Relaxed Breathing Method** and **Assertive Exchange** (see Chapter 8) will also help you to achieve success. For example, if you are living alone, with few friends and no family members to give you emotional support, your target could be 'to increase the number of social interactions that I have with people during the day'. To achieve this, your steps might include:

- Go outside the house, for a walk or an errand, every day.
- Smile at a minimum of three people and greet them if they look likely to respond.
- When standing in line to purchase food or other items, make small talk or exchange pleasantries with other customers.
- Go to the library or park and join groups if there are opportunities to do so.
- Seek out opportunities to volunteer or offer your services, especially at local community agencies, animal shelters, etc., where you are likely to be welcomed and included in the group.
- Give yourself small rewards and lots of encouragement for the efforts you are making.

The sense of alienation will not go away on its own. It takes interaction with people and your own efforts in challenging this tendency in your thinking. When you start to approach people again, be they strangers or your own friends or loved ones, be careful that you don't place too much weight on each single encounter so that it becomes an 'all or nothing' event! The term 'all or nothing' (Burns, 1980) means that (knowingly or unknowingly) you are putting the other person to the test. They must perform perfectly, according to your specifications, or you are likely to say to yourself: 'There! I knew it! People always let me down. It's just not worth trying. I'm never doing this again.' The result is that you give up, after the first (or a very early) try. Remember that very few things in life are immediately successful! Therefore it is very important that you persevere with your efforts and approach encounters with others without any prior expectations.

Dealing with the avoidance of intimacy is doubly difficult, because your partner is also unsure what to expect from you, just as you are unsure of what to expect from yourself. The tips on establishing a 'Healing Partnership' in Chapter 3 may be helpful reading for you both. Again, be wary of 'testing' your partner or your friends, by expecting them to 'prove' their caring for you. Such behavior is manipulative and assumes that you know what the other person is thinking, and what has influenced his or her behavior. Your assumptions might not be accurate so it is best to avoid such behavior.

Most of us, even at good times, experience fears of rejection, especially when we are establishing or re-establishing relationships. The fears may be connected to feelings of unworthiness or a certainty that if our partner found out what we were really like, he/she would leave us for sure! It is harder work to stay with a relationship and try to negotiate the bumpy parts than to walk out, in order avoid facing the bumps.

Try to face your fears, stop trying to take responsibility for everything that goes wrong, and dare to think of yourself as a worthy partner for someone. You need to discard any thoughts of yourself as 'damaged beyond repair'. Concentrate on whatever you can find in your relationship (with spouse, partner, friend, co-worker, etc.) that is positive, or is still working, and build from there. While you will need to acknowledge aspects of your trauma and talk about it some of the time, it is also important to have some periods of time together, however brief, that feel 'normal'. Try talking about mundane things – the weather, football, home decorating, an article in a magazine, etc. Despite the fact that your life has been turned upside down, you need to find a balance again in order to relax and enjoy other people's company.

10

Your Life before the Trauma

Stuck at the Time of Your Trauma

Too often, when people have lived through a catastrophic experience, their sense of the past and vision of the future stops – all that they can see in front of them are continuing pictures of the terrible tragedy that has befallen them. They begin to think and speak in extremes, such as 'I'll always feel like this!', 'I'll never get over this!' or 'I'm permanently damaged!'

The diagram on the next page can be used to explore how trauma can affect a person's whole outlook on present and future life. Think of the dark line in the middle of the diagram as a person's lifeline. It starts at birth and then moves on through a period of relative safety. During this time a person would have both positive and negative experiences – on the diagram, imagine these taking place anywhere in the oval background area either on the + positive or the – negative life experience area on either side of the lifeline. Although most people have to cope with some negative or difficult experiences, they would usually be strong enough or have enough resources to deal with these life experiences reasonably well. Their sense of safety, therefore, would have remained relatively intact.

However, at the time of trauma (illustrated here by a hollow circle in the negative life experience area) it is as if most of the person's energy gets stuck at that one place and continues to stay there from then on.

Energy Distribution after Trauma (Herbert & Jarisch, 1998)

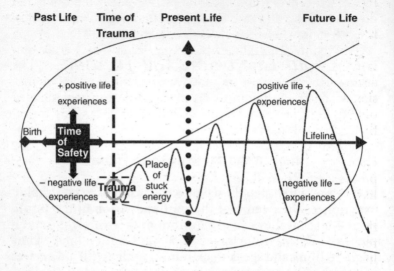

In other words, from the time of the trauma onwards all of this person's subsequent experiences, whether positive or negative, are overshadowed by the trauma. This is demonstrated by the curvy lines that emanate from the trauma circle, casting an ever-larger influence over this person's present and future life. People often describe this experience in words like: 'I am stuck at the time of the trauma', 'It is as if most of my energy stayed in that place', 'Everything in my life is clouded by the memory of the trauma'.

Even worse, the trauma seems to have blocked all access to this person's previous sense of relative safety in life. This is illustrated by the vertical, black broken line that runs through the trauma circle. It is almost as if the period before the trauma never existed.

If this represents how you have been feeling, or what you have been saying, to yourself or to others, it probably seems as if the trauma now defines the way you are, rather than you having any control over it. Just like the flashbacks discussed earlier, there is an *internal trauma imprint* that keeps repeating and does not allow you to see beyond the trauma, which is right in front of your face, all, or almost all, of the time.

This trauma imprint creates 'tunnel vision' – all you see now is interpreted through the terms of the trauma experience. The accompanying feelings of guilt, panic, shame, and/or depression, lead to a questioning 'Why me?' – a sense of being singled out by fate. You wonder if you are cursed or jinxed. You expect that things will never get better.

Until it is possible to feel connected with life again, your choices and your coping strategies will be very limited. Your problem-solving skills and your ability to make decisions are likely to be diminished too. So, what can be done?

It is important to believe that things *can* get better. While the trauma cannot be erased, it is possible to contain your reactions and begin to claim back much of your functional life. It may help to think of it as shifting your focus – not forgetting the trauma, but learning to see beyond it, or around it. The traumatic experience, and your reactions to it, will, with time and perseverance, move to a place on a 'shelf' in your memory, where you decide how and when you want to look at them.

Reclaiming Your Functional Life

Trauma therapists, both in Britain and North America, have found that drawing a chart of the stages or significant events in an individual's life *before* the trauma, is useful in helping people to reclaim a sense of meaning and purpose. This type of diagramming method has been called the Eriksonian 'Lifeline' exercise and originated thirty-five years ago in the writings of Dr Erik H. Erikson, a professor at Harvard University, and a leading figure in the field of psychoanalysis and human development. Erikson (1963) proposed that there were eight stages in the development of the human personality, and that an individual's movement or progression from one stage to the next could be charted by means of a diagram. He suggested that all development could be considered 'a series of crises', and that the critical steps in development, the turning points, were 'moments of decision between progress and regression'. He believed that individuals could move a bit forward and backward, and could repeat a stage if something happened to block their progress at that time in their lives.

We believe that Erikson's concept of growth over the span of life events implies that the human spirit will rise to new challenges and that traumatic experiences can be overcome. The next exercise is thus offered to help you view your life span as a whole, a total picture. By moving beyond the boundaries or tunnels in your vision that were created by your experience of the trauma, you can begin to recognize your strengths again. You will start to regain your functional life.

Introduction to the Climbing Chart Exercise

One of the aims of this exercise is to remind you that you have coped in the past and you are still coping with a lot now. Gently, cautiously, 'take a look' at the *whole* of your lifespan, beginning as far back as you can remember, and carrying forward *beyond your trauma* to the time now. It is important to recognize your achievements, and decide how to transfer them to the present. Try to ensure that you are not clouded in your views by a type of 'negative filter' (the opposite of 'rose-colored glasses') that becomes a way of looking for the worst in things or picking out all the bad things that have happened in your life and using them as evidence that somehow you 'deserved' the trauma.

Although it may seem that time has been standing still since your trauma, or that you are 'stuck' at this point in time, it is very important *to realize that this is an illusion*! Time has passed, and you have survived and, somehow, your life has kept moving. Therefore the point of this exercise is to take stock, to look back at the events that have shaped your life significantly, both positive and negative, and to see the patterns that emerged before the trauma took place.

Exercise 19: The Climbing Chart exercise

Part 1: Getting started on your Climbing Chart

On a large piece of paper (or with several sheets pasted end to end), draw a vertical line from bottom to top. Use this line as the centre. On either side of it – the right side for positive, or growth experiences, and the left side for negative, or 'held back' experiences – plot the events of your life. Start at the bottom, with your earliest recollections, and work your way to the top, where you see yourself now. With each dot or memory that you mark along the way, indicate: *What happened? How old were you? How did you feel about it at the time?* Any memory or event that was significant to you should be noted, for example, if you had a pet that died, or a favorite pair of red shoes that made you feel special when you were very young, etc. It does not matter if it was significant to (or even noticed by) anyone else.

You should allow yourself at least *two hours of private, uninterrupted time* to do this exercise. If you have photographs from childhood years or other mementoes, it may be helpful to look through them to help you remember. Do not be too concerned about remembering things in order, or very clearly. There may be long gaps in your chart, where you remember very little at all. While you continue the process of making the chart, however, you will probably find that other bits and pieces of memories will pop back into your mind and you can add new dots to mark these remembered events at any point. *Try not to edit or make judgements, just write them down as you remember them. Don't be too negative, or too positive, just report.*

continued on next page

If you become overly distressed while doing this exercise, stop! Put the material aside for awhile, and use your notebook as an outlet to write down your feelings. When you are feeling calmer, you can go back to the exercise, or complete it at another time. The intention here is to help you make sense of your life experiences and put things in some sort of order. You will find 'clues' from your past that will help you to contain your feelings now and strengthen your coping skills.

You will notice that when you start to connect the dots of your memories, the line around the centre begins to form a sort of spiral, like a vine climbing around a stabilizing pole. That is a very good image to keep in mind. Remember, all your life, things have happened to you, both good and bad, and you are still standing!

Traumatic experiences may have blocked you from accessing your inner strength, but it is still there, or you wouldn't have survived. Now, by reading this book and doing these exercises, you are trying to reconnect to your strength again. Don't despair if it seems to be taking a long time. If it was easy, you would have done it already, right at the start. One of the most important things to remember right now is to be patient with yourself!

continued on next page

We suggest that, after completing your chart, you let it 'rest' for awhile. Come back to it another time, when you have a private, uninterrupted hour or two to carry on with the interpretation part of the exercise.

The following example may help you get started:

– negative experiences   positive experiences +

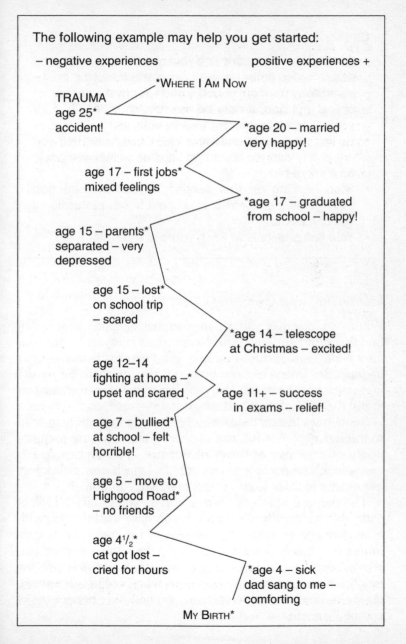

*WHERE I AM NOW

TRAUMA
age 25*
accident!

*age 20 – married
very happy!

age 17 – first jobs*
mixed feelings

*age 17 – graduated
from school – happy!

age 15 – parents*
separated – very
depressed

age 15 – lost*
on school trip
– scared

*age 14 – telescope
at Christmas – excited!

age 12–14
fighting at home –*
upset and scared

*age 11+ – success
in exams – relief!

age 7 – bullied*
at school – felt
horrible!

age 5 – move to
Highgood Road*
– no friends

age 4½*
cat got lost –
cried for hours

*age 4 – sick
dad sang to me –
comforting

MY BIRTH*

Cautions:

- If, while you were compiling your chart, you remembered and recorded other traumatic incidents from your past – particularly from childhood – such as physical abuse or sexual violation, it may be too difficult or upsetting for you to complete this exercise by yourself.
- Do not put yourself in harm's way if you sense that you are in any danger of hurting yourself or that you could be a danger to others!
- Stop working on this section, reread the reaction management strategies, and find a health professional you can talk to.
- Your first priority is to keep yourself safe!

Interpreting your Climbing Chart

When you look over your chart, you may be quite surprised to find that your 'climbing vine' has so many twists and turns. *You have really managed to cope with a lot over the course of your lifetime.* Regardless of how bothered you may still be by the memories of the trauma that you experienced, somehow you found the strength to live through it.

Sometimes the methods we use quite appropriately to help us through very stressful times become habits that are inappropriate or excessive at times of normal, everyday stress. For example, it's appropriate to run out of a large burning building, but not appropriate to run out of *every* large building!

The purpose of this section is to help you to take a look at your life and identify the methods you have used to cope with important events. However, you may or may not want to continue to use the same ways of coping in the future (for example, alcohol may be an old coping strategy that you now use too much, before you have given any other ways of coping a chance). It may become obvious to you that you now have better ways of coping than you did in the past.

Exercise 19: The Climbing Chart exercise

Part 2: Interpreting your Climbing Chart

A Ask yourself the following questions, as you look over your 'climbing vine' drawing. As you write down your answers (in your notebook), you will begin to recognize some repeated patterns of coping. You can *choose* whether you want to continue to behave in the same way.

1 How have I reacted to important events in my life?
2 How did I cope with positive events? And with negative events?
    (*Examples of possible reactions*: talking to others; getting angry or violent; tears)
3 Do I give myself credit for my accomplishments? How often?
4 When I am under stress, do I use a 'flight, fight or freeze' response? That is, do I either run away, freeze into inactivity or become very aggressive? Is this a pattern for the way I cope with everyday events? Is it successful?
5 Which ways of coping have been the most useful and successful for me in the past? How often do I use those now?
6 Has my coping pattern changed since the trauma? In what ways?
7 Are there some coping strategies that I know would be helpful that I haven't tried or don't use anymore?
8 How do I cope with people? a) those who are close to me? b) those who are strangers? c) those in some official capacity?
9 How do I cope when I am alone? Do I allow myself to be alone?
10 Do I take better care of others than I do of myself? In what ways?

continued on next page

Add any additional questions, that you think might be helpful, to the end of this list.

B Look at the answers you have written in your notebook and then see if you can make two lists:

   1 your helpful or positive coping strategies
   2 your unhelpful, outdated or negative coping strategies.

Now use this information to help yourself identify your common patterns of thinking and reacting.

When you work through the Climbing Chart Interpretation, follow these guidelines:

- Concentrate on shifting to the positive, and reducing the negative.
- Don't try to predict the future.
- This is an exercise to help connect you to the present by looking at what has come before.
- Just because things have always been a certain way, doesn't mean they have to stay that way.
- Do not minimize your strengths or achievements, or maximize your faults or shortcomings!

11

Guilt, Self-blame and Self-respect

Whatever the circumstances of your trauma, as you have worked through the preceding chapters in this book, you have probably found your feelings gradually shifting. For a while, you may have noticed only your fears or your rage, but as you found different ways to cope with those strong emotions, other feelings (like guilt, for instance) probably began to emerge from the shadows and demand your attention. The purpose of this chapter is to help you get a handle on these emotional reactions and begin to understand the level of responsibility you feel.

Survivor Guilt

For some people, guilt will be the emotion most strongly connected to their trauma, especially if there has been a death involved. At first, these feelings of guilt may be related to surviving when others have not. You may feel unworthy to have lived, when someone else, whose life you thought was very important, has died. Later on, you may feel guilty for beginning to enjoy yourself again. Engaging in normal social interaction, relaxing and temporarily forgetting about the past may feel like a betrayal of others who were lost or left behind or whom you consider to have suffered even more than you did. These are feelings of *blame* and you may try to take complete personal responsibility for the way in which you made your decisions before or during the trauma.

When family members or friends encourage you to come out with them or to try something new, you may react with anger at their expectation that you should be getting on with your life when, to you, that seems impossible. You may find that you avoid activities that you would have participated in without hesitation, like a neighborhood barbecue or your child's school sports day. Somehow now it doesn't feel 'right' for you to be there. Although you might put on a brave face, inside you feel as if you've been marked, or singled out in some way to permanently carry the burden of responsibility for the tragedy that has occurred.

Blaming Yourself

In your attempts to create meaning from what has happened, in other words, to make sense of what was senseless, there is a danger that you will develop a heightened degree of self-blame, holding yourself responsible for a tragedy over which you had no control.

It is a natural human tendency to want to find a reason for things. Very often, when there seems to be no other possible reason for a random occurrence, we think, in some way that it is our fault, that we *should* have been able to anticipate it or prevent it or, in some superhuman way, have been able to minimize the harm. Frequently, the standard of behavior we expect from ourselves in this respect far exceeds what we would expect from any other human being. The following exercise may help you to see if your guilt reactions are 'out of balance':

Exercise 20: The responsibility rating

Try, as objectively as possible, to determine the level of guilt that you are feeling by assigning it a number, from 0–10. For example, if you have *no* feelings of responsibility related to your trauma, or you are bothered very little by any sense of guilt, the number you choose would probably be 0 or 1 out of 10. If you are troubled by guilt *some* of the

continued on next page

---

time, but feel that other emotions are much stronger for you, your rating might be more or less in the middle, a 4, 5 or 6. If your guilt is so overwhelming that you dwell on it nearly all of the time, can't think of anything else, feel you are marked for life, then your rating would be 10.

Like the other emotional reactions we have dealt with, guilt is not static, but can be changed as a result of examining the underlying causes, the thoughts and beliefs related to it, and by trying out new ways of looking at things. Using the numerical rating will give you a way to gauge whether there has been any change in your feelings.

Write down the answers to these questions in your notebook:

1 How high is your level of guilt? Can you give it a rating out of ten? (Write down the number and today's date.)
2 Have you been able to talk about your guilt feelings with anyone? Are you keeping secrets? Are there some things you have not told anyone?
3 Do you blame yourself for things that others do not blame you for? (If yes, be specific in your answer.)
4 Do you dwell on the past?
5 Do you consider yourself responsible for what happened? To what degree?
6 Do you think that, by doing something differently, you could have prevented what happened?
7 Are you afraid to examine your guilt? Are you afraid to admit it to yourself?
8 Do you use a different standard for judging yourself than you do for judging others?
9 Are you ready to forgive yourself? To let go of some of the responsibility? *continued on following pages*

The Origins of Guilt

It may be puzzling that some people are more susceptible to a guilt response than others, but the answer often lies in their earlier, pre-trauma experiences. For instance, a common practice in child-rearing is inducing a sense of guilt in children as a means of teaching them the difference between right and wrong. While this may be necessary in order to pass on a moral code of conduct (for example, if they have injured another child deliberately, it is appropriate for them to feel guilty, in order to learn responsibility for their actions), unfortunately it often tends to be over-applied, even to simple mistakes or accidents. As a result, guilt is perhaps one of the most over-learned emotional responses (Thompson, 1993). Often the child ends up feeling responsible and guilty for anything bad or negative that happens to others around him or her. Gradually the child begins to view himself or herself as bad or negative, and the cause of misfortune for others, just by being there or by not trying hard enough to control what happens.

---

10 Was guilt a common feeling in your childhood experiences, and did it influence your early sense of yourself? What messages did you receive from your parents about your worth? About taking responsibility?

Sometimes parents who administer harsh punishments, or who abuse their children physically or sexually, will tell the child, 'You made me do this', 'If you weren't so bad, I wouldn't do this' or 'Now you're getting what you deserve'. Even though the child has been hurt and violated, at some level he or she starts to think that the parent must be right, and begins to take responsibility for the parent's abusive behavior, as if somehow he/she 'brought it on'.

---

11 Have you ever thought that abuse was your fault? Are you still taking all, or most of, the responsibility for others' bad behavior?

As children grow older, this pattern of reacting in a guilty manner begins to be more widely applied, sometimes to any new situations that the child or adolescent experiences. Fears of making mistakes and thus 'causing' everything to go wrong, may make the growing teenager overly watchful and perfectionistic in their outlook.

In adult life, men and women sometimes channel these feelings in different ways. Women tend to find themselves more often in caring roles, where they take on a great deal of the responsibility for others. For men, the feelings may be as strong, but may be masked by a super-conscientious work performance or a tendency to blame others to conceal their secret blaming of themselves.

---

12 Have you recognized any of your own patterns of behaving described in this discussion? As an adult, have you continued patterns that were established in your early years?

Obviously, guilt is a complex emotion. It keeps us stuck in the same patterns of reacting and generalizing over and over again. Guilt is often connected to secrets – things that we have been afraid to admit, even to ourselves.

---

13 What have you been keeping secret? Is there something, some bit of your traumatic experience, even a thought or a feeling that you have considered so terrible you could never tell anybody about it? Something that you are ashamed of or humiliated about?

14 Try to write it down, say it aloud (when alone), or even tape-record it, so you can hear it played back to yourself. Do this without making any judgements. Try to read or listen to it with the same level of understanding that you might offer to someone else, by standards that are less harsh than those you use for yourself.

The act of putting guilt *outside of yourself,* so that you can look at it more objectively, may help you to determine how much responsibility really belongs to you and how much was actually beyond your control or your ability to predict what would happen.

Layer after Layer

During the aftermath of a trauma, many people find themselves *ruminating* over what happened. Again and again, they blame themselves for what was done or not done, regret actions taken or generally feel responsible for it all. The disorientation and uncertainty that accompanies a trauma can act as a trigger for the guilt or the feeling of over-responsibility.

If the phrase 'dwelling in guilt' seems to describe how your thoughts are stuck, you may be looking at past situations or actions in the same way, over and over again. Just telling you not to think about it would *not* be helpful. You have the right to interpret your part in the traumatic experience as you see fit and there is no intention to minimize how profoundly you may be affected by what happened to you or to others. At the same time, you need to recognize that guilt is such a familiar emotional response that it can be over-applied to situations where things go very wrong. In this way, guilt becomes the surface emotion or the primary way you interpret your role in events.

If you think of your emotional reactions as having layers, like an onion, it might make sense to look underneath the 'guilt layer' and work out what other emotions you are experiencing. Is there a layer of anger? A layer of hurt? Are there layers of sadness, regret, confusion, despair? Try to identify as many other emotions as possible.

Looking at Guilt in a New Way

If guilt *is* a very familiar emotional response to you, then assuming that *you* are responsible for bad outcomes is likely to be the first conclusion you jump to. While you can't prevent your thoughts from going in that direction in the first place, you *can* keep yourself from stopping there and looking no further.

Try asking yourself: my natural response is to shoulder all the guilt, but what are four other possible ways of looking at what happened?

(One other possibility might be that you have only part of the responsibility; another might be that there was no way you could have predicted what was going to happen; a third might be that you did your best; a fourth might be that what happened was totally beyond your control.) Even if your guilt feelings remain very strong, keep working to find other realistic alternatives to think about. Use the 'four other possible ways of looking at it' strategy any time you are having a strong emotional response.

Reclaiming Your Self-respect

It is likely that you have lost a lot of your former confidence by going through the trauma. You may blame yourself for the way you reacted and consider yourself weak. Sometimes it is easier to take the blame than to acknowledge that some things just happen and are beyond our control. The idea that no matter what you do, how hard you try and how watchful you are, certain terrible events are bound to occur, can be a terrifying thought.

Ask yourself these questions before reading Nicole's description of her guilt feelings:

- If you let go of your guilt, acknowledged your humanness, forgave yourself, how would things change?
- What would stop you from doing this?
- Are you punishing yourself? Blaming yourself for not being super-human? Treating yourself as if you could have predicted the future?

'*I lost my husband Tim in a sailing accident. I still can't forgive myself that he is no longer here. We were both very experienced sailors and I had originally agreed to go with*

Tim on the trip that afternoon. However, some friends called by unexpectedly and Tim decided to go with my friend's husband, Pete, instead, so that the two of us could stay behind and chat. Pete was not an experienced sailor and when the boat unexpectedly got caught up in very strong crosswinds, he panicked and completely froze and couldn't do the things that Tim asked him to do to regain control over the boat. In the end Tim fell overboard after having been hit by the sail. Although Pete tried to save Tim, he could do little to pull him out from underneath the boat where he had got caught somehow. Tim had been knocked unconscious and then drowned. I just could not forgive myself that I hadn't insisted on all of us going together. The pleasant memory that I had of the afternoon with my friend was completely overshadowed by my feelings of utter self-blame and guilt. I feel that I am responsible for Tim's death, because I am sure this would never have happened had I been there. I feel that Tim died because of my selfishness and that I will never be able to forgive myself. Life is not the same without Tim and I shall never experience any joy again. Tim can't and therefore I don't deserve to!'

Nicole

You may have felt similar to Nicole after your own experience. These are very understandable and natural feelings and are linked to the human wish to be in control of one's life and destiny. Your thoughts that the trauma might not have occurred if only you had acted differently before or during it give you the illusion that you could have controlled the event. These thoughts make your healing and recovery process very difficult because they stop you from accepting and coming to terms with the trauma. You cannot rewrite history, no matter how you long to do so: disasters and accidents *don't* make sense and you cannot control or plan for them.

You have to acknowledge that under the circumstances you made certain decisions and, even if you had some doubts in your mind at the time, decided to follow a course of action. At the time you could not be certain of the outcome of the event, even if some part of you may have anticipated some tragedy. Until you allow yourself to accept that you cannot control your own and other people's destiny, much as you would like to be able to do so, you won't be able to heal properly. This is a very difficult concept to accept because it recognizes our vulnerability and fragility as human beings. By working to accept it, you may be able to connect to a deeper, more spiritual understanding of life.

Accepting Yourself

It may be very difficult to accept what has happened to you and it may be even more difficult for you to accept the person you have now become. There have been changes and your mind may be refusing to accept these changes. You might have found out things about yourself, through your actions or your lack of action or your reactions, that have appalled you.

One of the basic assumptions that most likely formed part of your internal 'bubble of safety' was the belief that, under severe circumstances, you would rise to the occasion and act wisely and well (Janoff-Bulman, 1985). Perhaps you expected that, if a bus came screeching around the corner with no brakes and out of control and a small baby was directly in its path, you would throw yourself in front of the baby? To some degree, we all expect the best from ourselves in extreme circumstances. *But what if that doesn't happen?* Often, how we react in a life-threatening situation is not the way we planned to or imagined we would.

In order for a situation to be considered traumatic, it must overwhelm the person's coping resources, involving a serious threat to their life or well-being, or the witnessing of such a threat, and it must leave the person feeling horrified, fearful or helpless. By this very definition, it is highly likely that you did not cope with your trauma in the way you anticipated that you would. Your body's automatic responses of 'fight, flight or freeze' took over. Perhaps you couldn't move, but instead stayed frozen to the spot, or maybe you ran away or broke down in fear and cried.

Whatever part of your reactions to the trauma you are feeling ashamed of and guilty about, it is likely to be the same part that makes it so difficult for you to accept yourself again. Your self-respect could be counted among the losses. If your self-respect has been destroyed by the results of your own actions, it is very important that you seek professional help rather than isolating yourself with your sense of self-hatred and retreating into self-abuse through drinking, banging your head or cutting yourself, taking illegal drugs or putting yourself in dangerous situations.

Learning to Live with Yourself Again

Accept the fact that you have come this far through your own valiant efforts and hard work. Now, in order to overcome and work through your guilt, try the following exercise. Write down as much information as you can in your notebook.

Exercise 21: Steps in managing your guilt feelings

Step 1 *Begin to separate the past from the present.* Recognize the difference between today, here and now, and what has already gone before. Write down those things that belong to the past and then start to notice what is around you in the here-and-now. When was the last time you really took notice of the here-and-now? Try to stop yourself from living in the past.

Step 2 *Examine your intention before the trauma.* (Mitchell, 1990) What were you really intending to happen that day? Did you set out with the intention of deliberately causing the harm that resulted? Were there circumstances beyond your control?

continued on next page

Step 3   *Even if a part of your mind did intend harm to come to someone, e.g. wanting an abusive spouse to be dead, can you acknowledge that you have other parts of yourself that are feeling remorse or are traumatized at the reality of what happened?*

Step 4   *Treat yourself with some compassion!*

Step 5   *Accept that you are only human.* Try and understand if there are some aspects of the trauma in which you expected superhuman qualities from yourself. Do not exaggerate your ability to predict or control the world.

Step 6   *Stop punishing yourself.*

Step 7   *Acknowledge your ability to be able to change for the better.* You can't make the trauma 'unhappen' but you can still decide to lead a life now that brings out your good qualities. Find and cultivate whatever is good in yourself.

Step 8   *Decide how best you can make amends* (Matsakis, 1992). Do something positive for someone else – donate community service or contribute to a memorial in some way.

Step 9   *Allow yourself to feel self-respect again and begin to live in a way that is worthy of that respect.*

12

Grief, Loss, Sadness and Emotional Pain

Coping with Loss

Your traumatic situation might have involved the death of a loved one or an injury to yourself that resulted in a temporary or permanent change to your body or perhaps the loss of your personal sense of safety and security. Whatever your experience, it is important to acknowledge the loss you have experienced and allow yourself to grieve properly.

When you completed Exercise 19, the Climbing Chart, in Chapter 10, you might have been surprised to notice that many of the significant events from childhood to adulthood on your chart involved the loss of something. It is not at all uncommon to feel shattered by a loss and to have difficulties coming to terms with the fact that someone or something that one was very attached to is gone from one's life. While the death of a friend or loved one is a bereavement that is obvious to everyone, there are many other kinds of loss that can also affect a person deeply but might not be acknowledged as real experiences for grieving, for example: a miscarriage, still birth, being made redundant, the break-up of a relationship and divorce. If you have experienced any of these or a similar personal loss, you may find it hard to cope with the lack of recognition of your pain by others. Exercise 22 asks you some questions about the losses that you may have had and how you have coped with these in the past.

Exercise 22: Your own experience of loss

Counting the losses

Identify in your notebook how many and what type of personal losses you have experienced in your life so far. You could do this by going over your notes from Exercise 19 in Chapter 10. Remember that these should be events that involved a feeling of loss for *you*; do not be influenced by what others thought about these events. These are your personal experiences and feelings.

Coping with your losses

Now answer the following questions in your notebook:

1 How have you coped with your losses in the past? Did you just 'get on with things' or did you acknowledge your sadness and give yourself space to grieve?

2 Did you make some type of memorial gesture to mark the loss? What was it?

3 If these losses involved death, did you attend funerals or other ceremonies marking the passing away of this person?

4 Which loss has been the hardest for you? Why did it feel this way?

5 Are there other things you still need to do to honor the loss, now that some time has passed?

6 You may have done some things to comfort yourself, like eating too much or spending money on presents for yourself that weren't really necessary, but that helped you to feel better for a short time. People commonly use such coping strategies to get them through a time of grief. What was particularly helpful to you when you were trying to cope with a loss?

7 What was not helpful about your coping behavior? Did you turn away from others or toward them? Did you try to share with others what the loss meant to you?

8 Are there any things that you would have done differently, with hindsight?

If the loss has been significant, most people will experience feelings of shock and disorientation immediately after the event. Sometimes this is accompanied by a brief or a prolonged period of denial ('It didn't really happen...'; 'He is not really dead!'; 'I keep waiting for him to come through the door...'). The loss feels too painful to admit and therefore we tend to resist believing it for as long as possible. Another way of coping is to diminish the loss ('It wasn't really that important!; 'I'll be fine!'; 'He (or she) is much better off...' or to deny our own feelings ('I'm not upset...nothing's changed!'). This can also manifest itself as a shutting off of *all* emotion; the bereaved person will go about making practical arrangements for funerals or taking care of the family as if they were functioning quite automatically, like a robot. On the inside, they may be feeling numb and untouched by what is happening around them; their faces may look blank and they are unable to cry.

- Did you experience any of these feelings? Are they still with you?
- What do you have a hard time admitting, even now, about your loss?
- Has the reality of your loss sunk in? Is that very hard to cope with?

When the reality of the loss *does* sink in, it is common for people to feel very angry toward others – including those who have been directly involved – as well as at well-wishers who make unhelpful or insensitive comments. If someone close to you has died, you may even have secretly felt angry toward that person for leaving you and then ashamed and guilty for having felt that way. Actually it is very normal to be angry for a while with the person who has died and left you in so much pain.

- Have you experienced angry feelings that you are now ashamed of?
- Are those feelings preventing you from moving on and dealing with your loss?
- Have others made stupid comments about your loss? What were the worst things that were said to you?

Make a list of comments made to you in your notebook and see if you can channel your frustration into a feeling of amazement at how dense people can be! Then put this list away for a while, knowing that you have acknowledged your difficulties and coped with them.

Feelings of anger may gradually give way to *despair and depression*. Feeling deeply sad, you may have withdrawn from social contact, either physically, by cutting yourself off from other people, or emotionally, by putting on a brave face and pretending that all is well. Inside, though, you have been feeling miserable and isolated. When you are in such a frame of mind, it often seems that things keep going wrong. Everyday problems, such as having the car in front of you take *your* parking spot, become very stressful when added to the major loss you are struggling with. Your 'personal shield' feels very thin and you may start to wonder if life is worth living.

- Do you recognize these feelings?
- Can you identify everyday stresses that have felt like too much to cope with as you struggled with despair?
- What else has gone wrong?
- Will you make a deal with yourself to choose to see this life through, at least a good while longer, and actively protect yourself from any drastic actions now until you feel able to cope again?

All of these emotional reactions are normal stages of the grieving process that most people pass through (though not necessarily in the same order) after experiencing a significant loss. The length of time will vary from individual to individual; grief has its own timetable, one that is often quite different from society's idea of how long it *should* take to recover from a tragic loss.

Problems may arise, however, if you get stuck at one stage and can't allow healing and resolution of the loss to occur. An example of this would be refusing to acknowledge that a loved one is really gone, by keeping a living 'memorial' – continuing to set a place at table, refusing to change the arrangement of their possessions and maintaining everything 'exactly as it was'.

When a person is grieving, they may feel reluctant to let go of their painful loss and begin to enjoy their life again, for fear that they would be betraying the memory of the person or of the thing that was lost. They may feel unable to say goodbye and may torment themselves about things that were left unsaid or undone. They may also worry about appearing to others as if they had not really cared about that person or that situation.

- Did you recognize any of your own feelings or behavior as you were reading through this section? If so, describe them in your notebook.
- What is preventing *you* from healing and resolving your loss?

> While you are working on these questions, give some thought to the type of commemorative or 'goodbye' ritual that would be personally meaningful to you. This would have to be one that would help you to honor and acknowledge the depth of your loss and then move on. Think of ways you have said goodbye in the past that you might have forgotten to use for your traumatic situation.

Memorial Rituals

Here are a few ideas for memorial rituals that other people have found helpful:

A Night to Remember

Spend an evening looking at photographs or clippings. Allow yourself to cry, have some pleasant memories, think about the things you miss and the things you don't miss. Put your photos in order in an album or folder and label them with the date and time and whatever else you remember about the occasion. Make this night very memorable: have a special candle burning and use aromatic scents, such as sage, sandalwood or rosemary, fragrances that are often used for commemoration. Or you could have the person's favorite perfume or aftershave around you. Buy some flowers, play some music that you and the lost person may have liked. Celebrate the time you were able to share together with this person.

Writing a Special Letter

Write a letter to the person who has died (or left you behind), saying on paper all the things you would have liked to have said to him or her were they still alive. Tell that person what you have been through, what he or she meant to you and what you are going to do now to get on with your life. Allow yourself to experience all feelings that need to come out while you are writing this letter; they are part of the grieving and natural healing process. 'Send' the letter by burying it in a significant place, burning it and scattering the ashes or by depositing it near the person's remains. In the case of a very recent death, the letter could also be enclosed in the coffin.

Group Memorial

If you are part of a group that has experienced a traumatic loss, the group can have a ritual of 'letting go' together. For instance, each member could write a personal goodbye message which is inserted into a helium balloon and then all the members of the group release their balloons at the same time and watch them rise and disappear into the air.

River of Life

Another ritual, called the 'river of life', can be carried out individually or as part of a group. It involves making small paper boats that each contain a candle and an individual message. The candles are lit, and the little boats are set afloat in a large stream or river. This can also be done with flowers or some other significant or symbolic object. Messages are attached and the objects are then set afloat.

Keep notes in your notebook as you work through your own grief and loss. When you are ready, proceed with your own 'goodbye' healing ritual. There are also some useful books listed in the resource section at the end of this book. If you feel really stuck and your feelings of loss don't seem to be shifting, seek some professional help.

13

Changes in the Body, Physical Pain

Learning to Live with the Physical Scars of Trauma

When your body has been injured and the trauma has left permanent physical changes, you will need time to heal from the emotional scars as well as the physical scars. Complete healing from the physical injuries may indeed not be possible, but *in order to move on with your life and make it livable again, you need to learn to find ways to accept and get to like your new self.* That this is not an easy task goes without saying, as Antonia describes:

'For me the hardest was to learn to live with (yes and even love!), my changed physical self. I had been a model and my whole livelihood was dependent on my perfect body image. The trauma was a road traffic accident, in which my boyfriend Allen drove our Mercedes Coupe into a large tree, after coming off the road round a very sharp bend under icy driving conditions. Allen broke both his legs and had various other fractures, on his arms and ribcage, but otherwise his body image remained intact. Things were worse for me. A branch had come through the window on my side of the car and caused a serious large cut right across my face. It also tore off one of my arms, so that it had to be amputated later. Friends and family were relieved that I had survived and told me so in the hospital. I couldn't share their feelings. I felt I would rather have died than look like this. I hated my swollen face with the huge scar running across it. I looked completely grotesque, like a monster out of Frankenstein, and certainly not like me anymore! Even worse

was the complete loss of my left arm. It is not possible to put into words the heart-wrenching pain I felt at the loss of this. I have to honestly admit that there were several times when I really felt like ending it all. I hated everything – Allen for not having prevented it, the world for being such an unjust place and most of all myself! I could see no purpose in living anymore, I had lost everything, there seemed no reason to carry on, there really seemed no point!

What stopped me? I think somewhere inside me was a tiny voice that urged me not to give up, to stay strong. Although this voice was very small and quiet, it was strong enough to put me in touch with that part of myself that felt I would be wrong to kill myself. I had to completely re-adjust. I had to change most of my social circle. I no longer belonged to the glamorous and glitzy 'showbiz' world. I went back to college to retrain as a business administrator. Gradually, as I stopped avoiding people all the time, I learned that people responded positively to my personality. People seemed to like my open yet sensitive manner. I learned that aside from my previously beautiful body I had other qualities that had not been destroyed by the trauma. I had never really noticed these other sides of myself and I now think nobody else really valued them before the trauma. After all, I had lived in a world that was more about image rather than personal qualities. I also found a new partner, Luke, who helped me a lot toward learning to accept myself. Luke was somebody with whom I could share all my feelings. He understood my anger and rage and my feelings of loss, sadness and despair. He also taught me to appreciate a different kind of beauty, other than the one that concentrates purely on physical image. I learnt to appreciate the beauty of human friendships, I rediscovered my talent for painting. By taking up walking I learned to appreciate the beauty of all the elements around me. My sense of self changed completely.

All this happened very gradually and was by no means always easy. For example, I often automatically did things that would require the use of my left arm. Although I do carry a prosthesis now, I can no longer use that arm. It took me a long time to accept that I would never get my normal arm back and I some-times still really miss it. It has got much easier though and I can say that I even love myself again!"

Antonia

Antonia's account demonstrates how damaging the effect of trauma can be, but also that it *is* possible to enjoy life again, even if this means a complete change of life circumstances. Indeed, adjustment to the physical injuries caused by a trauma often demands those changes in your life; it may no longer be possible for you to go back to your previous work or to pursue the old hobbies or sports that you may have enjoyed before the trauma. As in Antonia's case, your circle of friends will often change, too. People frequently say that during a crisis your true friends emerge. People often find that those whom they thought of as friends before the trauma turn out not to be true friends, and yet new, more understanding friends emerge instead. Some-times, because of the physical injuries, there can also be a real sense of isolation, because you may not be able to get about as much or as easily as you did before your trauma.

So, the first step toward learning to live with the physical scars is often to *accept* that you will have to make certain changes in your life. The next exercise is designed to help you look at those areas of your life you may need to change.

Exercise 23: Identifying your areas of change

1 Take your notebook and write down all the things you used to be able to do before the trauma. Then give yourself a score anywhere between 0 – 10 for your past quality of life (where 0 = poor and 10 = very high quality of life).

2 Now write down all the things that you are doing now. Again give yourself a rating anywhere between 0 – 10 for your present quality of life.

continued on next page

---

3 Calculate the difference between your score of past quality of life and your score for present quality of life and make a note of this. What do you notice? Did you expect there to be such a difference in scores? Is this discrepancy really justified? Or would you like to try to redress this unequal balance? (Or maybe you are one of the few people who have already mastered this and the scores are not all that different after all!)

4 Now write down all the changes that you would like to make to help increase your present quality of life. Of course, these need to be realistic and to take into account any changes in physical condition. Nevertheless, there are probably many things that you could be doing despite the physical changes, that so far you have not tried. Give yourself an estimated rating between 0 – 10 for your quality of life if you really managed to make these changes. Would you be satisfied with this score? If not, maybe you could think of some further changes you would like to try.

5 Order the changes that you have listed in terms of how easy you think they would be to achieve. Select the easiest change first and write down in your notebook what you have to do to achieve this first change and how and when you will have done this.

6 Try to work towards the easiest changes first and once you have mastered them, advance to the more difficult ones in your own time. It might be helpful if you could get a partner or friend to help you achieve those changes.

Also don't forget to re-rate your quality of life at intervals and remember the challenge is to improve quality of life, regardless of the physical changes you have experienced!

Learning to Accept Your Body as It Is Now

Now that you have begun to work on reinstating quality into your life despite the physical changes it would also be helpful if you learned to reconnect with your body and reintegrated the hurt or changed parts with the rest of your body. Your goal is to learn to accept your body and your self as it is now.

After severe physical injury it can be difficult to accept the changes to your body image and to start to see yourself as a whole person again. It is quite understandable that you find it hard to accept your new self and your altered physical image. However, your old body image *has* changed and now you need to give yourself a chance to get to know and familiarize yourself with your new body image.

The following exercise is designed to help you with this, but take as much time as you need and only work on this when you feel ready. It gives you the opportunity to explore your present body as it is, in order to welcome and learn to accept each part of yourself.

Exercise 24: Reclaiming your body

1 The task is for you to reclaim each part of your body separately. Start with those parts of your body that you feel either positive or neutral about (do not choose any parts that carry any negative feelings for you), for example you could choose to start with your elbow or your wrist (if those parts of your body haven't been changed by the trauma and you don't feel negative about them).

2 Set aside 5 or 10 minutes every day and work on your chosen part of the body. When you were a baby you spent hours just looking, touching and exploring each part of your body in order to get to know and to familiarize yourself with them. Just as when you were a baby, allow yourself to discover that chosen part of your body all over again. Examine how the skin looks, is it smooth or rough? Allow yourself to feel it, touch it, stroke it. Think about its function and how it has served you over the years that you have been together. Do this every day for the next three days.

continued on next page

---

3 By day 3 start writing a letter of appreciation about this part of your body. Acknowledge what a wonderful functional part of your body this is. Write down all that you appreciate about this part of your body, make friends with it.

4 On day 4 allow yourself to buy a small, inexpensive present for this part of your body, for example, some cream or oil, a feather or a ribbon. It should be something that you can put on it , use to stroke it with or even give it a little massage, to show your appreciation and care. Let it know in that way that you accept it as a part of yourself.

5 When you are ready to like and accept this part of your body, move on to other parts of your body until you feel ready to learn to accept those parts that have been damaged by the trauma. When you are ready, go through the steps of this exercise as you did with all other parts of your body. Allow yourself to really get to know those injured parts, to look at them closely, to feel them, to touch them and in your own time to welcome them back as part of your own body by proceeding to Steps 3 and 4. In your letter of appreciation you may also recognize how brave that part of your body has been and how hard it must have been to be rejected and unloved for so long. Explore, if you can, ways to love or like this part of your body.

Remember: those damaged parts are with you now in this way because your body *has* accepted them after the trauma. So, it is not your body but your mind that has rejected them! Your task now is to help your mind to find ways of befriending and accepting them as part of your new whole being.

Learning to Live with the Pain

When physical pain following injuries becomes chronic and persistent it can seem like an inescapable and constant reminder of the trauma. At this stage there may not be any medical solutions to remove your pain completely, but you can still learn ways of controlling the pain, rather than it controlling you and your life.

> 'Although I recovered reasonably quickly from the two operations, following the fractures to my hip and upper thigh, it was this constantly gnawing pain that was crippling me. It seemed to be worse every time I moved and subsequently I withdrew more and more from doing anything. Claire, my wife, was a keen walker but even when she asked me to come out with her to take a stroll through town I refused. Eventually, I ended up staying mostly at home, doing very little but sitting and eating, which started to have its effect on my weight. I felt very miserable about myself. In the end Claire had had enough. She sought advice from a friend, who was a physiotherapist. Together they got me onto a program where very slowly I learned to increase my activity levels again. I now feel so much better. The pain hasn't stopped, but at least I am not just sitting about like a "couch potato" any longer, but I am actually doing things for myself again. Even if I am slow, it is better doing something, than nothing at all!'
>
> *Joe*

If you are suffering from chronic pain and feel that it has taken over your life, the following exercise might be helpful:

Exercise 25: Taking control of your pain

1 If you are suffering from chronic pain, ask yourself how many activities you have stopped doing because of the pain.
2 Ask your partner or another person who knew you well before the trauma what they have observed you giving up as a result of the pain. Make a note of all those activities that you have lost in your notebook.

continued on next page

---

3 Now look at your list of lost activities and decide whether there may not be one or two of these that you could modify so that with time you might be able to manage them despite your pain?

4 Write yourself a program to help you towards achieving this.

For example:

Aim: To walk into town again.

   a. Work out how many steps you can manage presently, (e.g. 300 steps).

   b. Next, decide what number of steps you would like to have increased your mobility by for the next week. Decide on a small increase, e.g. 350 steps.

   c. Now practise walking a little more every day until by the rest of the week you have mastered 350 steps. Congratulate yourself if you manage this. If not, try again for another week, until you have achieved this goal.

   d. Then work out what your aim for the following week is and continue in *small* steps until you have mastered your aim of walking into town.

   e. Once you have achieved your first aim, set yourself another aim to work toward.

5 If you can't identify anything from your list of lost activities that you would like to work toward, think of an activity that you haven't done in the past but that you would like to be able to master. Proceed in the same way with small incremental steps.

Now that you have taken steps to control your pain rather than allowing it to take over your life, you could explore some additional techniques to help you manage and feel more in control of your pain.

Exercise 26: Imaginative transformation of the pain

1 When you next experience a pain, ask yourself the following questions:

  a. If your pain was a shape what shape would it be?

  b. Would it be smooth or rough? Are the edges round or jagged?

  c. Would it be solid or liquid?

  d. Imagine yourself touching it. What would it feel like?

  e. Would it be hot, warm or cold?

  f. What color would it be?

  g. If it could make a noise, what noise would it make?

  h. How loud would that noise be?

  i. Now notice its size. How big is it?

  j. Whereabouts in your body is it? Right inside or more on the periphery?

2 Now explore how to change its image.

  a. Think of how your pain's image would need to change in order for the pain to be less intense and powerful.

  b. If you could change its color to a more healing, soothing color what would it be?

  c. If it could change its shape and size, how would you do this?

  d. Imagine it turning into a liquid and flowing out of your body.

  e. Imagine changing it into lots of little parts, which are less intensive and painful than the big shape of pain that you first pictured.

continued on next page

f. Explore any change of the image that is different from the original image that was associated with your pain. Another example would be for you to imagine healthy cells fighting and conquering the pain, with the pain running away.

3 Allow yourself to be as open and as explorative with your image as you like. People often find that the less they concentrate on the actual physical sensation of the pain, the less they notice it and the more likely it is that some of the pain intensity can be reduced. *In order to achieve this it is important that you make your image as strong and powerful as you can.*

4 Practise this exercise as often as you can (several times a day). Give yourself a rating between 0–10 for pain intensity (0 = no pain, 10 = the worst you have experienced), one when you first notice the pain and another rating again after you have done this exercise.

Use your notebook to start a pain diary, in which you record each time you use this exercise. Give yourself time and be patient – don't expect the exercise to work the first time – but keep sticking with it!

It might also be very helpful for you to practise relaxation on a regular basis. Start using the breathing exercises that are described in Chapter 8 of this book.

Finally, recognize that your decision to take more active control over your pain is a very positive one and the first big step toward mastery.

14

Healing, Letting Go and Moving On

'The world breaks everyone
and afterward
some are strong
at the broken places.'

Ernest Hemingway, *Farewell to Arms*

Recovery is a lengthy process. Individuals vary, both in their reactions to traumatic events and in the amounts of time they need for different stages of the healing process. By the time you come to this chapter, you might feel that your healing has begun and that you are moving along the path towards recovery, even though there is still a very long road ahead.

The human spirit seems to be able to find new strength in the aftermath of terrible events and eventually triumphs over adversity. Whether you are ready now or many months from now, you can begin to think about a future for yourself and start to visualize where you would like to be, when you have moved beyond your traumatic experience.

Visualizing the Future

Visualization is a very powerful tool in the healing process. There are many stories from the medical community about people who have greatly enhanced their recovery or far exceeded anyone's expectation for their health by *visualizing* themselves getting better. This is not meant to be a substitute for following

Managing Traumatic Stress

good medical advice or an excuse to avoid therapy but an additional tool. In the safety and privacy of your own imagination, you can create an image of how you want things to be in your future. Use the exercise below to help you with this.

Exercise 27: Visualizing your future

Read through the instructions a few times to familiarize yourself with the steps before carrying out the visualization exercise. It can be repeated as often as you wish. You can also tape-record the instructions or have someone read them to you, so that you don't have to keep looking at the page.

1 Settle back in a chair where you can sit comfortably, with your back supported. Allow yourself to begin to relax slightly. Take a few deep breaths. With each breath, exhale fully and bring the next breath in more deeply, into your diaphragm. Feel your belly pushing OUT as you breathe in fully and pulling IN as you exhale completely. *Listen to your breathing*. Let distracting thoughts or sounds around you just pass by – you don't have to attend to them for a moment. Close your eyes now and let any excess tension begin to drain away – from the top of your forehead down past your neck and shoulders, down your arms and hands and OUT through your fingertips. Let any excess tension in the lower part of your body drain away now, down your tummy and thighs, past your calves and ankles, and OUT through your toes. Enjoy the feeling of being calm and relaxed.

2 Now, begin to see yourself as you would *like* to be, the way you *want* to be, in the future. Imagine that you are surrounded by a golden-blue light, which signifies the state of your well-being. Look around you. What kind of place are you in? What are you doing? What colors can you see around you? Are there sounds? Are the sounds

continued on next page

clear? Soft? How are you feeling? See and sense yourself with a new self-respect and a new understanding of yourself. You are accepting yourself more fully than ever before, discovering courage and strength you didn't know you had. Enjoy this feeling of arrival. Feel at peace with yourself. Stay with this feeling for a while. When you are ready, come back to the room you are in and *know* that you have the strength to move forward in your life.

This visualization technique may be repeated as often as you wish. It is intended to bring you a sense of calm and comfort during your journey to recovery.

Forgiveness

There might be some pressure from others, or from yourself, to forgive those who might have had some part in your traumatic experience. It is equally likely that you are holding on to some feelings you have not been able to forgive yourself for. Forgiveness is a very difficult issue to come to terms with. Premature forgiveness, especially toward those directly responsible for harming you, may be detrimental to your healing. It may feel as if you are being pressured to say that something is okay, that it doesn't matter any more, when that is very far from the truth of how you really feel.

Try, then, to think about forgiveness in another way. Rather than excusing a behavior or an action or erasing it from your memory, think about 'forgiveness' as permission to move forward a little, into the present. *You are not forgetting what happened but, instead, accepting that it did happen.* In this way you are letting go, a little at a time, of the feelings that have kept you stuck. *You are allowing yourself to experience life today as a little bit freer from the past.*

You can still proceed with any search for justice that you are involved in, but you needn't feel you have to wait for that process to be finished before you can heal. Your sense of outrage, your trauma experience – that you have been looking at in the same way for so long – can be 'put' into a mental container, just like a box on a shelf. It has not gone away, but it has a place to rest for a while. You decide when you want to take it out and look at it again. This shift in attitude will help you to forgive yourself and work to accept yourself as you are now, and to live more in the present.

Anniversary Dates

Even for people who feel they are well on the way to resolving their traumatic experiences or their losses, an upcoming 'anniversary' of the event can have an extremely unsettling effect. You may be taken by surprise, especially if you feel you have 'dealt with' your reactions. You may not expect to find yourself suddenly depressed or agitated again, unable to concentrate or even beginning to have dreams or flashbacks once more. The researcher Bessel van der Kolk explained this succinctly, saying, 'the body knows the score' (1994). In other words, our subconscious seems to mark time and, when it gets close to the anniversary date, presents us with a series of reminders.

If some of your post-trauma reactions have returned with intensity around an anniversary time, this does not signify that you are 'not dealing' with your trauma. It should *not* be viewed as a backward step in your healing. Instead, try to look at anniversary reactions as one more natural step in your recovery. Once you have a framework for understanding what is happening to you, your reactions become more predictable and you can begin to feel more in control.

The two weeks or so leading up to an anniversary date are likely to be the most difficult period, in terms of the return of traumatic reactions. Your anxiety level rises, as the date becomes closer and associated feelings are recalled. Once the trauma anniversary has passed, you will probably notice a dramatic reduction in symptoms. Although you may have been very upset and agitated, it probably won't take you long this time to feel your normal self again.

Anniversary reactions can be managed, to reduce their impact. It is a good idea to plan some sort of symbolic ritual that will be personally meaningful to you, to help you mark the occasion. This could be as simple as lighting a candle at a particular time of day, or taking a moment of silence (alone or with others), making a donation (of money or of your volunteer time) to a particular cause, attending a church service, taking a walk in the park, requesting that a meaningful piece of music be played on a radio program, etc. The point is that you choose an action, no matter how small, that allows you to acknowledge what has happened and pay tribute to the person or thing that has been lost. In this way, too, you honor yourself for having come this far in your life, in spite of the trauma.

Native American Indians used a form of a 'blessing ritual' for such occasions, described in the book, *Good Grief Rituals* by Elaine Childs-Gowell (1992). This ritual consisted of gathering a candle, a bowl of water and some sage, the herb that is traditionally associated with wisdom. At the time or in the place you have chosen to mark the anniversary (this might be outdoors or indoors) you light the candle, dip your fingers in the water and touch your forehead, saying, 'Bless my forehead, that I may understand fully'. Next you dip your fingers in the water and touch your eyes, saying 'Bless my eyes, that I may see clearly', then you touch your lips with the water, saying 'Bless my lips, that I may speak the truth', then you dip your fingers in the water and touch your heart, saying 'Bless my heart, that I may carry strength and courage'. Now the sage is crushed between your fingers, and you inhale its pungent smell, then you wash your fingers in the bowl of water. The water is poured away, while you pause and reflect for a moment, and then the candle is blown out.

Your Healing Experience is Unique to You!

Not everybody needs professional help to recover from a traumatic experience (Herbert, 1996). Recovery means that you have been able to integrate your traumatic experiences into your everyday life and although the memory of it has not gone, you are able to think about your experiences without feeling over-whelmed and out of control. The length of time it takes you to reach this stage will be particular to you. Every person differs in their own experience of a trauma, even if all the people at the time of the event were in exactly the same position. Likewise, each person's path to recovery is unique. However long it takes you, the most important point is that you allow yourself to recover in your own time and don't feel pushed by the expectations or advice of others.

Seeking Professional Help to Support Your Healing Process

Despite all your efforts, there may be times when you feel you are 'stuck' and you just can't seem to move beyond the trauma on your own (look back to the Energy Distribution Diagram in Chapter 10, p. 126). This is an indicator that you would probably benefit from professional help. It is not a sign of weakness, and in fact this recognition that you might need outside help is a sign of your own personal strength. It indicates that you are able to take personal responsibility for your recovery and that you recognize your own limits and boundaries.

Certain forms of therapy have been found to be very effective in helping people recover from trauma. However, it is important that you find yourself a professional who really understands trauma and who is properly qualified and registered with a professional body.

Finding the Right Professional Help

You can seek appropriate help from either the National Health Service (UK only); a private insurance scheme; the legal sys-tem (if you are entitled to compensation for the damages you suffered); or by finding yourself a registered private psychothera-pist who is experienced in this area.

Often, the best starting point is to visit your medical practi-tioner. He/she should be able to advise you on the services that are available in your local area. Most medical practitioners can recommend therapists, such as clinical psychologists, psychiatrists, clinical nurse specialists, community psychiatric nurses (CPNs) or others, who might be able to help you heal from the trauma. Again, it is extremely important that you seek help only from a professional who has been properly trained and has experience in the area of traumatic stress reactions.

Even if you find that your medical practitioner isn't very supportive or doesn't seem to understand, don't give up! Try a different one until you find one you're comfortable with.

Many public services can only offer limited therapy time to you and sometimes they can have very long waiting lists. If you feel that a long waiting time would be very difficult for you to manage, you should discuss this with your therapist and also your medical practitioner. There may be a priority treatment service for certain difficulties or they may be able to suggest other alternatives for you while you are waiting.

Alternatively, if you can afford to pay for yourself or have a private insurance plan, you could see a private therapist. Your medical practitioner may also be able to recommend recognized therapists that work privately in your area. A register of approved and qualified psychotherapists is available from the United Kingdom Council for Psychotherapies (UKCP) and also from the British Association for Behavioral and Cognitive Psychotherapy (BABCP). The British Psychological Society (BPS) also publishes a register of all Chartered Clinical Psychologists or Chartered Counselling Psychologists. The British Association for Counselling (BAC) should be able to recommend suitable trained counsellors or counselling agencies in your local area. The Eye Movement Desensitization and Reprocessing (EMDR) Association for the UK and Ireland also has a list of their approved and registered members, but be sure to check that the recommended person is also suitably qualified and registered with one of the other above bodies.

Although this can seem a bit overwhelming at first, it is very important that you ask for as much information as possible. Don't just accept things at face value. It is perfectly acceptable to ask professionals about their experience and qualifications. If they are properly registered and qualified they will be more than happy to show you their relevant certificates. If you don't feel comfortable with a therapist, trust your own feelings! You won't progress with your process of recovery if you feel that you can't have an honest, open and trustworthy relationship with your therapist.

Finding the Right Type of Therapy

There are so many types of therapy available, it can be very confusing to decide on what might benefit you most. Research has shown that Cognitive Behavioral Psychotherapy (CBT) or Cognitive Therapy (CT) – which uses similar approaches and methods to the ones that we have been using in this book – seem to be very effective therapies for treating post-trauma reactions. In addition your therapist might be trained in a method called Eye Movement Desensitization and Reprocessing (EMDR), which is also increasingly used alongside other therapeutic approaches, such as CBT or CT. More detailed research of the use of this method is currently beginning to emerge; EMDR was specially developed to be used with people who have been traumatized (Shapiro, 1995) and patients seem to be reporting increasingly that it has been effective and helpful to them.

There are also some alternative therapies available that you might want to consider in conjunction with your psychotherapy, for example, aromatherapy massage, homeopathy and craniosacral therapy may be very helpful in supporting your therapeutic healing process. Again, be very careful to use qualified, registered and reputable practitioners.

Whatever type of therapy or therapist you decide on, you might find it very helpful to use some of the exercises or suggestions in this book *with* your therapist during your recovery process.

Marking the Journey You Have Made

Lastly, whether you have traveled your path of recovery on your own or with friends or a partner or with the help of a Professional, the final stage is to mark the journey that you have made in a personally meaningful way.

Expressing your story through some artistic means can be a powerful healing tool. Even though you may have never done anything 'artistic' in your life, and are convinced that you have no creative talent, this exercise can still be valuable. Many trauma survivors have found that writing or creating something to represent their ordeal symbolically was a vital step in their recovery.

Compiling a scrapbook of clippings and photos, finger-painting, wood-carving, drawing a series of sketches, painting in crayon or watercolor or oil, writing a short story, composing a poem, making an audio- or videotape, are all creative ways of telling your story. But they are by no means the only ways to use – even painting a sign is an artistic task, if the intention is to help you in your healing.

Here are a few suggestions to get you started:

1 The 'Breathing Line'

When you start to explore methods of creative expression, it is best not to be too concerned about the finished product. Just pay attention to what your senses tell you to do. The book *Managing Traumatic Stress Through Art* by Cohen, Barnes and Rankin (1995) suggests that, as a start, you pick up a pencil and draw a line to represent your breathing. Your line(s) might be short or long (quick breaths or deep breaths), curved or straight, flowing or broken. Use the **Relaxed Breathing Technique** you learned in Chapter 8 to help you attend to your breathing. As the rate of your breathing becomes slow and relaxed, you may wish to draw it with your eyes closed. By producing a simple line drawing, you are showing, on paper, how you have mastered your traumatic stress reactions through control of your breathing.

2 'Imprint of Fear'

Another exercise suggested by Cohen, Barnes and Rankin is called the **Imprint of Fear**. Select or mix several strong paint colors to represent your fear. Combine the colors you have chosen to form an abstract painting of the feelings of fear you experienced, both during and after your trauma. In a variation of this exercise, you could use the bold colors of fingerpaints to make handprints, which you place on top of each other, in different positions.

3 *Collage*

The collage method has been used successfully by Falklands War veterans who received post-traumatic stress therapy at the Royal Naval Psychiatric Hospital in Haslar. A collage can be made by pasting together clippings, photos, magazine cuttings/ pictures or other substances, like cloth, sand, dried flowers, etc. on a hard surface such as cardboard or poster board so that the result depicts your traumatic experience. A collection of the collages produced by military personnel treated at the Haslar Hospital was exhibited some years ago by the Manchester Art Gallery. The images and emotional struggles depicted in these collages were vivid and powerful. Whatever your artistic inclinations, you *can* cut and paste and use color and texture to create a collage that depicts your journey out of trauma.

Try not to put off this task: it will help you express in a complete and genuine way the impact of the trauma on your life. Let it be a final healing task that allows you to make sense of things so that you can put them to one side. Or, if you choose, it could become a more public expression that you might share with family or friends or significant others. It is a unique way to tell others what it is like to live through chaos and put yourself together again. It symbolizes the completion of your journey.

In the words of the poet, Sheenagh Pugh:

Sometimes our best efforts do not go
amiss; sometimes we do as we meant to.
The sun will sometimes melt a field of sorrow
that seemed hard frozen: may it happen for you.

(from 'Sometimes')

A Final Note

Congratulations! By the time you read this page you may be well on the road to recovery. You might have come quite a long way already, with the path ahead of you now visible again. Equally, you might feel that you have only just started to make the first tentative steps in the direction of recovery, and you might still be considering if you can find the courage and strength within yourself to make this journey.

Wherever you currently are on your journey, we would like to encourage you to try and keep moving along at your own pace.

It may be hard, but if you persevere, in the end the effort will definitely have been worthwhile!

References

American Psychiatric Association (APA) (1994) *Diagnostic and Statistical Manual of Mental Disorders*, 4th ed., Washington, DC.

DSM–IV Classification of PTSD:

Condition 1: The person has experienced, witnessed, or been confronted with an event or events of actual or threatened death or serious injury, or a threat to the physical integrity of self or others.
Condition 2: The person's response involved intense fear, helplessness, or horror.

Bass, E. and Davis, L. (1988) *The Courage to Heal: A Guide for Women Survivors of Child Sexual Abuse*, Perennial Library, Harper & Row, New York
Bower, S. A. and Bower, G. H. (1976) *Asserting Yourself: A Practical Guide for Positive Change*, Addison-Wesley, Reading, Mass.
Burns, D. D. (1980) *Feeling Good: The New Mood Therapy*, Avon Books, New York
Breathnach, S. B. (1995) *Simple Abundance: A Daybook of Comfort and Joy*, Warner Books, New York

Charlton, F. (1992) *Coping With Panics*, Patient Education Pamphlet, Traumatic Stress Clinic, Middlesex Hospital, London

References

Childs-Gowell, E. (1992) *Good Grief Rituals: Tools for Healing*, Station Hill Press, New York

Cohen, B. M., Barnes, M-M. and Rankin, A. B. (1995) *Managing Traumatic Stress Through Art: Drawing from the Center*, The Sidran Press, Lutherville, Md.

Dolan, Y. M. (1991) *Resolving Sexual Abuse: Solution-focused Therapy and Ericksonian Hypnosis for Adult Survivors*, W. W. Norton, New York

Erickson, E. H. (1963) *Childhood and Society*, 2nd ed., W. W. Norton, New York

Green, (1994) 'Incidence of PTSD', handout presented by Figley, C. R. at Training Workshop: *Trauma & Loss: Integrating the Theoretical and Clinical Components of Grief and PTSD*, in Toronto, Canada, December 1996

Herbert, C. and Jarisch, U. (1998) 'The use of Energy Distribution Monitoring to affect schema-shifts in trauma', presentation at the *Annual Conference of the European Association for Behavioral and Cognitive Therapies* in Cork, Ireland, September 1998

Herbert, C. (1996) *Understanding your reactions to trauma, a booklet for survivors and their families*, Psychology Department, Warneford Hospital, Oxford

Hodgkinson, P. E. and Stewart, M. (1991) *Coping with Catastrophe, A Handbook of Disaster Management*, Routledge, London

Horowitz, M., Wilner, N., Alvarez, W. (1979) 'Impact of events scale: a measure of subjective stress', *Psychosomatic Medicine*, vol. 41, 209–18.

Janoff-Bulman, R. (1992) *Shattered Assumptions, towards a New Psychology of Trauma*, The Free Press, New York

Janoff-Bulman, R. (1985) 'The aftermath of victimization: rebuilding shattered assumptions', in Figley, C. R. (ed.) *Trauma and Its Wake: The Study and Treatment of Post-Traumatic Stress Disorder*, Brunner/Mazel, New York

Manchester City Art Galleries (1988–9) *The Falklands Factor: Representations of a Conflict*, art exhibition, 10 December 1988 – 22 January 1989, Manchester, England

Matsakis, A. (1992) *I Can't Get Over It: A Handbook for Trauma Survivors*, New Harbinger, Oakland, CA

Meichenbaum, D. (1994) *Treating Post-Traumatic Stress Disorder, A handbook and practice manual for therapy*, Wiley, Chichester

Mitchell, J. T. (1983) 'When disaster strikes … The critical incident stress debriefing process', *Journal of Emergency Medical Services*, vol. 8 (1), 36–9

Mitchell, J. T. (1991) 'The relationship of guilt to intention', personal communication at workshop training session, Critical Incident Stress Certification Training, Edmonton, Alberta

Pugh, Sheenagh (1990) 'Sometimes', *Selected Poems*, Seren, Wales

Rose, S. and Bisson, J. (1998) 'Brief early psychological interventions following trauma: A systematic review of the literature', *Journal of Traumatic Stress*, vol. 11 (4), 697–711

Saakvitne, K. W. and Pearlman, L. A. (1996) *Transforming the Pain, a Workbook on Vicarious Traumatization for Helping Professionals who Work with Traumatized Clients.*, W. W. Norton, New York

Sanford, L. T. (1990) *Strong at the Broken Places: Overcoming the Trauma of Childhood Abuse*, Avon Books, New York

Selye, H. (1946) 'The General Adaptation Syndrome and the disease of adaptation', *Journal of Clinical Endocrinology*, 6, 117

Shapiro, F. (1995) *Eye Movement Desensitization and Reprocessing, Basic Principles, Protocols and Procedures*, The Guilford Press, New York

Sheehan, P. L. (1994) 'Treating intimacy issues of traumatized people', in M. B. Williams and J. F. Sommer, Jr. (eds.), *Handbook of Post-Traumatic Therapy*, Greenwood Press, Westport, Conn.

References

Thompson, J. (1993) 'The origins of guilt', personal communication, Traumatic Stress Clinic, Middlesex Hospital, London

Tyler, P. (1998) 'Upsetting Things', PTSD assessment scale for clients, personal communication, Psychological Services: Clwyd, Wales

Van Der Kolk, B. A. (1994) 'The body keeps the score: Memory and the evolving psychology of post traumatic stress', *Harvard Review of Psychiatry*, 1, 253–65

Wegner, D. (1989) *White Bears and Other Unwanted Thoughts: Suppression, Obsession and the Psychology of Mental Control*, Viking, New York

Woodward, S. H. (1993) 'Sleep disturbance in Post-Traumatic Stress Disorder', *PTSD Research Quarterly*, vol. 4, no. 1

Useful Books and Addresses

Useful Books

For Post-traumatic Stress Disorder

If you want a less extensive, readable guide on understanding trauma:

Claudia Herbert (1996) *Understanding your reactions to Trauma: A booklet for survivors of trauma and their families.*, The Psychology Department, Warneford Hospital, Oxford OX3 7JX , UK
This book has also been translated into Japanese and is published (1999) in Japan by Hoken Dohjinsha, Inc., 2–12–2 Fujimi, Chiyoda-ku, Tokyo, 102–8155, Japan

A comprehensive and more detailed self-help book for both single-incident and prolonged, repeated traumas (like childhood sexual abuse):

Aphrodite Matsakis (1992, 2nd edition 1996) *'I can't get over it'* – A Handbook for Trauma Survivors, New Harbinger Publications, Inc., Oakland, California, USA

Three further useful and topical books:

Aphrodite Matsakis (1998) *'Trust after Trauma'*, – New Harbinger Press, Inc., Oakland, California, USA

Aphrodite Matsakis (1999) *'Survivor Guilt – a self-help guide'*, New Harbinger Press, Inc., Oakland, California, USA

Dena Rosenbloom and Mary Beth Williams (1999) – *'Life after Trauma' – A Workbook for Healing*, The Guildford Press, New York, USA

For Loss and Grieving

The following is a really good little resource book:

Elaine Childs-Gowell (1992) *A Healing Companion: Good Grief Rituals, Tools for Healing*, Station Hill Press, New York, USA

For Sexual Difficulties

This book could be helpful to share with your partner:

Lonnie Barbach (1983) *For Each Other: Sharing Sexual Intimacy*, Corgi, London, UK

Cognitive Therapy

A readable yet comprehensive book, which contains much useful information and exercises:

David D. Burns (1989) *The Feeling Good Handbook*, Penguin Books, London, UK

Another useful book that explains many helpful strategies that can be used to change the way you feel:

Dennis Greenberger and Christine A. Padesky (1995) *Mind Over Mood – Change how you feel by changing the way you think*, The Guildford Press, New York, USA

Eye Movement Desensitization and Re-processing (EMDR)

If you want to know more about this increasingly commonly used method for trauma therapy:

Francine Shapiro and Margot Silk Forrest (1997) *EMDR: The Breakthrough Therapy for Overcoming Anxiety, Stress and Trauma*, Basic Books, New York, USA

For further professional self-help material on a mail-order basis:

The Oxford Stress and Trauma Centre on www.oxdev.co.uk

Useful Addresses

United Kingdom

There are a number of specialist trauma services available, both within the National Health System and privately. Your first port of call should be your medical practitioner, who should know what resources are available in your geographical area.

These two services specialize in working with traumatized people:

For referrals within the National Health Service:

Traumatic Stress Clinic
73 Charlotte Street
London W1P 1LB
Tel: 020 7436 9000

For clients seeking help privately:

The Oxford Stress and Trauma Centre
8a Market Square
Witney
Oxon OX8 7BB
Tel: 01993 779077
Website: www.oxdev.co.uk

Other organizations that may be able to advise on Registered Trauma Specialists:

The British Association for Behavioural and
    Cognitive Psychotherapies (BABCP)
General Office
PO Box 9
Accrington BB5 2GD
Tel: 01254 875277

The British Psychological Society publishes a register of all approved Chartered Clinical Psychologists. Many of these will have undergone the necessary training to be able to help you:

The British Psychological Society (BPS)
St Andrews House
48 Princess Road East
Leicester LE1 7DR
Tel: 0116 254 9568

The United Kingdom Council for Psychotherapies also publishes a register of approved and qualified psychotherapists, some of whom may specialize in trauma work:

United Kingdom Council for Psychotherapies (UKCP)
167–169 Great Portland Street
London W1N 5FB
Tel: 020 7436 3002

USA

This association maintains an international list of skilled crisis responders, therapists, trainers, debriefers and others.

Association of Traumatic Stress Specialists (ATSS)
7338 Broad River Road
Irmo, SC 29063
Tel: 001 803 781 0017

This is the national professional organization for psychologists, which will be able to give you details about the psychological association in your state. Your state psychological association will be able to refer you to practicing psychologists in your area. However, you should ensure your therapist has experience in working with trauma.

American Psychological Association
750 First Street, NE
Washington, DC 20002-4242
Website: www.apa.org

The International Society for Traumatic Stress Studies publishes a directory of all their members, located across the world, most of whom are trauma therapists and may be able to help you:

The International Society for Traumatic Stress Studies (ISTSS)
60 Revere Drive
Suite 500
Northbrook
Illinois 60062
USA
Tel: 001 847 480 9028
Website: www.istss.org

Anxiety Disorders Association of America
6000 Executive Boulevard
Rockville
Maryland 20852
Tel: 001 301 231 9350

American Academy of Experts in Traumatic Stress
Website: www.aaets.org

Canada

In Canada each province has its own association of certified (licensed) psychologists. Contact numbers and addresses can be obtained from:

The Canadian Psychological Association
151 Slater Street
Suite 205
Ottawa
Ontario KIP 5H3
Canada
Tel: 001 613 237 2144

Canada Association of Psychologists of Nova Scotia
Website: www.3.ns.sympatico.ca/apns

Canadian Traumatic Stress Networks
Website: www.ctsn.rcst.can

Index

Index

Index

Appendix

Appendix

Exercise 1

Rate your strength of distress on the following scale:

0	1	2	3	4	5	6	7	8
No distress		A little distress		Definite distress		Marked distress		Severe distress

Date:_____ Time:_____

Time	Intrusive Memory	Sensations in your body	Strength of Distress (0–10)	Able to tolerate it	Push it away

Exercise 1

Rate your strength of distress on the following scale:

0	1	2	3	4	5	6	7	8

No distress · A little distress · Definite distress · Marked distress · Severe distress

Date:_____   Time:_____

Time	Intrusive Memory	Sensations in your body	Strength of Distress (0–10)	Able to tolerate it	Push it away

Exercise 3

A. Recognize the triggers:	Record your observations:
1 When did it happen?	
2 What were you doing at the time?	
3 What else was going on when it started?	
4 Was anybody else with you?	
5 Can you recognize any similarities between your current situation and the situation that you were transported to in your flashback?	
6 Can you remember when you have felt this way before?	
7 What is similar and what is different to the previous situation/s?	
8 What do you think triggered it? (For example, thoughts, smells, sounds, pictures, feelings, taste – or reminders such as conversations, media or special events, such as anniversaries.)	

B. Identify the traumatic memory:	Record your observations:
1 What do you remember about your flashback?	
2 Even if it feels a little distressing, describe in as much detail as you can what went through your mind.	
3 Can you describe or draw the images that you saw during your flashback?	
4 Do you know how long it lasted?	
5 Were you noticing what was going on around you or did the flashback block everything else out?	

Rate your strength of feelings on the following scale:

0	1	2	3	4	5	6	7	8
No distress		A little distress		Definite distress		Marked distress		Severe distress

C. Get to know your body's responses:	Record your observations:
1 What sensations did you notice in your body during the flashback?	
2 Try and describe them in as much detail as you can.	
3 How strong were these sensations? Can you try and give them a rating between 0 to 8 (using the above scale)?	
4 What were your thoughts about these sensations?	
5 How did you react and respond to those sensations in your body?	
6 What actions did you take to make yourself feel better?	
7 Can you think of other ways you may have used to control flashbacks in the past?	

Exercise 3

A. Recognize the triggers:	Record your observations:
1 When did it happen?	
2 What were you doing at the time?	
3 What else was going on when it started?	
4 Was anybody else with you?	
5 Can you recognize any similarities between your current situation and the situation that you were transported to in your flashback?	
6 Can you remember when you have felt this way before?	
7 What is similar and what is different to the previous situation/s?	
8 What do you think triggered it? (For example, thoughts, smells, sounds, pictures, feelings, taste – or reminders such as conversations, media or special events, such as anniversaries.)	

B. Identify the traumatic memory:	Record your observations:
1 What do you remember about your flashback?	
2 Even if it feels a little distressing, describe in as much detail as you can what went through your mind.	
3 Can you describe or draw the images that you saw during your flashback?	
4 Do you know how long it lasted?	
5 Were you noticing what was going on around you or did the flashback block everything else out?	

Rate your strength of feelings on the following scale:

```
0     1     2     3     4     5     6     7     8
●─────────────────────────────────────────────●
No          A little      Definite      Marked       Severe
distress    distress      distress      distress     distress
```

C. Get to know your body's responses:	Record your observations:
1 What sensations did you notice in your body during the flashback?	
2 Try and describe them in as much detail as you can.	
3 How strong were these sensations? Can you try and give them a rating between 0 to 8 (using the above scale)?	
4 What were your thoughts about these sensations?	
5 How did you react and respond to those sensations in your body?	
6 What actions did you take to make yourself feel better?	
7 Can you think of other ways you may have used to control flashbacks in the past?	

Exercise 5

Flashback Recording Chart

Rate your Strength of Responses on the following scale:

0	1	2	3	4	5	6	7	8
No distress		A little distress		Definite distress		Marked distress		Severe distress

Date/ Time	Trigger (external and internal)	Traumatic memory (content)	Your reactions (physical & emotional responses), Rate their strength (0–8)	Duration of flashback

Exercise 5

Flashback Recording Chart

Rate your Strength of Responses on the following scale:

0	1	2	3	4	5	6	7	8
No distress		A little distress		Definite distress		Marked distress		Severe distress

Date/ Time	Trigger (external and internal)	Traumatic memory (content)	Your reactions (physical & emotional responses), Rate their strength (0–8)	Duration of flashback

Appendix

Exercise 6: Avoiding the triggers

List of Triggers to avoid:	My plan of what I can do to avoid them:

Appendix

Exercise 6: Avoiding the triggers

List of Triggers to avoid:	My plan of what I can do to avoid them:

Exercise 7: Categorizing your triggers

Least difficult   most difficult

1 Triggers that I might be able to handle now	2 Triggers that I can't cope with yet, but I may be able to handle soon (maybe in a few weeks' or months' time)	3 Triggers that seem really hard to gain control over at the moment, but that I would eventually like to tackle	4 Triggers that I will always want to avoid (for my own and others' safety)

Exercise 7: Categorizing your triggers

●━━━━━━━━━━━━━━━━━━━━━━━━━━━━━━━━━━━━●

Least difficult   most difficult

1 Triggers that I might be able to handle now	2 Triggers that I can't cope with yet, but I may be able to handle soon (maybe in a few weeks' or months' time)	3 Triggers that seem really hard to gain control over at the moment, but that I would eventually like to tackle	4 Triggers that I will always want to avoid (for my own and others' safety)

Exercise 11: Keeping a sleeping log

Copy this log into your notebook or onto your computer. Use it every day during your sleep-monitoring period and remember to fill it out about 15–20 minutes after waking.

Day	Bedtime routine used:	Before I went to sleep I felt (indicate score by circling one from 1 = very tense to 5 = very relaxed)	I went to sleep at time:	During the night I woke at (time):	Action taken to get back to sleep:	I stayed awake for (minutes/ hours):	This morning I woke at:	When I woke up, I felt (indicate score by circling one from 1 = not rested at all to 5 = well-rested):	The following helped me with my sleep last night:
Monday		1 2 3 4 5						1 2 3 4 5	
Tuesday		1 2 3 4 5						1 2 3 4 5	
Wednesday		1 2 3 4 5						1 2 3 4 5	
Thursday		1 2 3 4 5						1 2 3 4 5	
Friday		1 2 3 4 5						1 2 3 4 5	
Saturday		1 2 3 4 5						1 2 3 4 5	
Sunday		1 2 3 4 5						1 2 3 4 5	

Notice those strategies which seem to be helpful and those that don't have a positive effect on your sleep. Discard the unhelpful ones and keep the helpful strategies. In this way, build up your own individualized sleep restoration program.

Exercise 11: Keeping a sleeping log

Copy this log into your notebook or onto your computer. Use it every day during your sleep-monitoring period and remember to fill it out about 15–20 minutes after waking.

Day	Bedtime routine used:	Before I went to sleep I felt (indicate score by circling one from 1 = very tense to 5 = very relaxed)	I went to sleep at time:	During the night I woke at (time):	Action taken to get back to sleep:	I stayed awake for (minutes/ hours):	This morning I woke at:	When I woke up, I felt (indicate score by circling one from 1 = not rested at all to 5 = well-rested):	The following helped me with my sleep last night:
Monday		1 2 3 4 5						1 2 3 4 5	
Tuesday		1 2 3 4 5						1 2 3 4 5	
Wednesday		1 2 3 4 5						1 2 3 4 5	
Thursday		1 2 3 4 5						1 2 3 4 5	
Friday		1 2 3 4 5						1 2 3 4 5	
Saturday		1 2 3 4 5						1 2 3 4 5	
Sunday		1 2 3 4 5						1 2 3 4 5	

Notice those strategies which seem to be helpful and those that don't have a positive effect on your sleep. Discard the unhelpful ones and keep the helpful strategies. In this way, build up your own individualized sleep restoration program.

LIBRARY, UNIVERSITY OF CHESTER